Midwife
FOR SOULS

SPIRITUAL CARE FOR THE DYING

A pastoral guide for hospice care workers
and all who live with the terminally ill

REVISED EDITION

by Kathy Kalina

auline
BOOKS & MEDIA
Boston

Nihil Obstat: Reverend Timothy Shea, S.T.L.
Imprimatur: ✠ Seán Cardinal O'Malley, O.F.M. Cap.
        Archbishop of Boston
        October 23, 2006

Library of Congress Cataloging-in-Publication Data

Kalina, Kathy.
  Midwife for souls : spiritual care for the dying / by Kathy Kalina.
— Rev. ed.
    p. cm.
  Originally published: St. Paul Books & Media, © 1993.
  Includes bibliographical references.
  ISBN 0-8198-4856-5 (pbk.)
  1. Caregivers—Religious life. 2. Hospice care—Religious aspects—
Christianity. 3. Terminal care—Religious aspects—Christianity. I. Title.
  BV4910.9.K35 2007
  259'.4175—dc22

                                        2006033299

The Scripture quotations contained herein are from the *New Revised Standard Version Bible: Catholic Edition,* copyright © 1989, 1993, Division of Christian Education of the National Council of the Churches of Christ in the United States of America. Used by permission. All rights reserved.

English translation of the Apostles' Creed by the International Consultation on English Texts.

Cover design by Rosana Usselmann

Cover photo by Mary Emmanual Alves, FSP

Published by Pauline Books & Media, 50 Saint Paul's Avenue, Boston, MA 02130-3491. www.pauline.org.

Printed in the U.S.A.

Pauline Books & Media is the publishing house of the Daughters of St. Paul, an international congregation of women religious serving the Church with the communications media.

8 9 10 11 12 13   23 22 21 20 19

Let us love
  with the urgency of the dying
    and the innocence of the newborn.

Let us love
  with the abandon of adolescence
    and the certainty of adulthood.

Let us love
  generously and openly
    taking all risks—
      for as we have been loved,
        we must love in return.

And in the love that redeems us,
  we open our hands and hearts
    gathering a bouquet
      to offer to heaven.

KATHERINE MARY KRSAK

Contents

APPENDICES

Foreword

MIDWIFE FOR SOULS IS A BOOK on hospice care, but it is much more than that. It is a "how to" for family members, friends, and hospice professionals involved in caring for terminally ill patients as they enter into the phase of their last moments, when life slowly ebbs away and death releases the soul to go home to God. These last days or hours are very difficult for family members, who often watch helplessly by the loved one's bed, not knowing what to do or say.

The author is a nurse, but she is also a deeply spiritual person writing from her personal experience. Kathy Kalina makes no apologies for being "one hundred percent Catholic," but her deep understanding of what human beings go through as their lives come to an end makes the book useful to everyone regardless of religious preference. It is written in a style that is both poetic and beautiful as well as practical and credible. It talks about how powerful prayer can be; it talks about how important it is for hospice caregivers to be attuned to this God if they are to be effective "midwives for souls."

I highly recommend this book for all who care for the dying whether as professionals, friends, or family members. The many stories of peace and joy coming into people's lives, even in the last few moments before death, point to why euthanasia must never be an alternative for anyone. Hospice care relieves pain and suffering–physical, psychological, social, and spiritual–so that patients can face the end of their lives in peace and with dignity. Just as midwives help mothers deliver a child, so hospice caregivers help the soul as it is "born into eternal life." It is a sacred mission; it is a true vocation. I rejoice that a book on the "Spiritual Care of the Dying" has finally been written.

JOSEFINA B. MAGNO, M.D.
President, International Hospice Institute

Preface

I HAVE COME TO BELIEVE THAT there are no accidents. My dear friend Dodie urged me to become a hospice nurse, and I assisted at her death in that capacity six months later. I'll never forget sitting beside her bed as she told me that she had no intention of dying, thank you very much. Inspired by the grace that abounds at such times, I told her, "I am here as the midwife of your soul."

I don't think I've ever prayed harder in my life, and I don't think I've ever felt such spiritual strength. Twelve hours later, with an expression that radiated wonder and peace, Dodie was born to eternal life. What could have been an unbearable loss became a joyous homecoming, and Dodie's parents were able to say that their thirty-four-year-old daughter had a beautiful death.

I went to Dodie's house with "head knowledge," but I left with "heart knowledge." Dodie's death transformed me into an apprentice midwife. I am still an apprentice.

Patients and families are my teachers, and I will not graduate from this school until my own death. So I will share what I know as one apprentice to another.

Even though I'm writing this book primarily for nurses, especially when beginning this work, I hope that those who want to serve as midwife for loved ones will also find it helpful.

Acknowledgments

Special Thanks

To the countless hospice workers who shared their stories with me;

To the patients and families who allowed me to be a part of their stories;

And to my parents, for showing me what a family can be.

ONE

❧ • ☙

Hospice Care

The Dignity of the Dying

I FELT CALLED TO HOSPICE WORK quite some time before I stopped whispering, "Wrong number!" Because of my hospital nursing experience, the thought of death conjured images of a slow, agonizing process, involving a helpless patient and a hopeless staff. It involved inflicting pain on already pain-racked bodies. I'm still haunted by memories of tying patients down to keep them from pulling out tubes, repeatedly sticking IVs into worn-out arms, and assisting with heroic resuscitative measures that we called the "million dollar send-off."

When I provided this type of "care" for the dying, I had the same sick feeling as when I participated in the hospital "care" of women in childbirth. Even though I knew the academic and legal rationales for distasteful practices, it never felt right.

Many times families would tell me, "We want everything done for our mother." I would shake my head, thinking, "They just don't know what *everything* is." Doctors have a tendency to think of death as a personal enemy, and that's usually good. If I have an illness that can be cured, I want my doctor to wage all-out war against it. But once it becomes evident that treatment is not going to be successful, I want to spend my last days in comfort and peace.

I can understand why it's hard for doctors to turn about-face at this point, but it hurts my heart to see patients put through the rigors of treatment, even such drastic measures as artificial ventilation, because the doctors hate to fail. My friend Dodie, for instance, was encouraged to start another round of chemotherapy three days before she died.

Fortunately, more and more doctors are referring their patients to hospice care when a cure is unattainable. And more and more families are asking for, even demanding, hospice care when that point is reached.

Hospitals are wonderful, necessary resources for the treatment of disease. But they are not the best places to die. Even if there are no painful treatments, the routine alone robs patients of control and peace. The focus is not directed to the comfort of the patient; it's directed to the convenience of the staff and the overall efficiency of the operation.

Vital signs are taken every four hours, baths are given every morning, meals are served at predetermined times—and the patient has no control over this routine. Staff members come in the room throughout the day and night, carrying out a variety of tasks at their convenience. There is often some limit on visitors. And patients usually hurt, because doctors and nurses have been taught that pain cannot be eradicated, just made a little easier to bear.

In contrast, hospice care is focused on the control of symptoms instead of the cure of disease. Pain is unacceptable, not a necessary evil. And pain medicine is given in pain-free ways.

The patient is consulted and included when decisions are made regarding a care plan, and the family helps provide that care. Our tools are primarily our hearts and hands, instead of high-tech equipment. Death is neither hastened nor prolonged.

Hospice care is loving support for patients who are living their last days and for their families. This support is physical, psychological, and spiritual. The hospice team consists of nurses, doctors, social workers, home health aides, clergy, and volunteers, and their roles often overlap.

The first hospice in the United States began in 1974, but true hospice care is not new to this country. Care for the dying has traditionally been a function of the family, with generous community support. Nursing duties were the woman's responsibility, and this art was passed down from mother to daughter. Hospitals were places for the homeless and the poor. It wasn't until the 1930s and 1940s that medical advances made hospitalization an attractive alternative to home care for all illnesses.[1]

In the days when medical care was geographically inaccessible, however crude it might have been, families surely felt the helplessness of being unable to provide treatment

---

1. V. Bullough and B. Bullough, *The Care of the Sick: The Emergence of Modern Nursing* (New York: Prodist, 1978).

for the dying. Today we have sophisticated and accessible treatment, but once those options have been exhausted, families are made to feel helpless in providing even basic comfort measures. Hospitals push families aside and, at best, treat them as guests. We are led to believe that death is a medical event best attended by experts.

The Death Event in a Fragmented Society

Probably the greatest cause of our perceived helplessness is the fragmentation of our families and communities. Because our families are scattered geographically, we no longer feel capable of caring for our own during a final illness. There is no Granny living around the corner who carries a lifetime of experience in her hands. There is no aunt nearby to share stories about sitting up with the dying. Frequent moves have left many of us without Church or community ties. Instead of a doctor who is almost a member of the family, we receive our health care from a multitude of specialists.

The hospice team can help fill these gaps, acting as a substitute for family wisdom and community support, giving families the courage to care for their loved ones at home. We can provide expertise, but must avoid assuming the superior role of experts.

I heard of one eighty-year-old gentleman who had been referred to professional counseling by some well-meaning person. He attended one session, came home, and said, "I think that's for people who don't have families." I believe that in-patient care of the dying should be reserved for people who have no caregiver or home, or whose care simply cannot be managed at home.

Since so many people hold full-time jobs, providing around-the-clock care can be a formidable undertaking. But I have seen families find creative solutions and make heroic sacrifices to give their loved ones the opportunity to stay at home. Adult children often take turns providing care, using vacation days or even taking a leave of absence from their jobs. Sometimes a circle of friends will rotate care days. When a spouse is the care-giver, relatives and friends can assume weekend duty to provide a much needed rest. I've seen such novel solutions as employers and even divorced spouses stepping in to assume the patient's care.

As the hospice movement grows, more and more people have come to experience firsthand the beauty of allowing the patient to live those last days surrounded by the comfort of home and family. And I'm seeing nurses with hospice hearts making the last hours better for patients and families in intensive care units, emergency rooms, and medical/surgical wards.

But I see a danger in hospice care in the United States— a danger that seems to be related to our society's devotion to and dependence on experts. There is the temptation to put our hospital-based, paternalistic model of care into practice even in hospice care programs. There is also the tendency to focus solely on the body while ignoring the spirit. This could easily lead to a hospice system that is only a notch or two above the expert-controlled, disease-focused hospital care of the dying—a care system that is often spiritually bankrupt.

Midwifery for Souls: Birthing to Eternal Life

Hospice care in the context of midwifery for souls is closely aligned to traditional midwifery in childbirth: a natural, gentle approach to an intimate and life-changing family event, with careful attention throughout the process to the body, mind, and spirit of the patient as well as to the family.

I have a friend who is a midwife, and I accompanied her on prenatal visits and home births from time to time because the symmetry between natural birth and natural death fascinated me. From beginning to end, the physical, psychological, and spiritual similarities are striking.

First, there's the shock of diagnosis. Even when a woman is trying to get pregnant, the news is unbelievable. And even though we all know that we must someday die, we really don't expect it to happen to us.

The next step is to consult professionals, seeking a good outcome. The pregnant woman absorbs information from veteran mothers, searching for the best way to make this journey. The terminally ill person reads articles and consults survivors, searching for an angle the doctors might have missed.

The last several weeks are a time of spiritual searching and life review. The pregnant mother works on relinquishing her pre-baby life, and the dying person detaches from this world.

The pregnant mother nests. She gathers all the things she'll need for the baby and prepares her home for the new arrival. The dying person carries out a reverse nesting, giving away belongings, putting business in order, and perhaps making funeral arrangements.

The pregnant mother wonders how she'll make room in her heart for someone else to love. The dying person wonders how to let go of loved ones.

The pregnant mother may feel out of control, as if her body has a mind of its own. The dying person may see the body as the enemy.

As the time of birth approaches, the mother worries about the actual birthing. *Will it hurt? Will I have the people I want around me? What will it really be like?* The dying person has the same questions.

Giving birth is something the body knows how to do, and usually does quite well if interventions are kept to a minimum. In the dying process, the changes in the body are self-protective. Medical interference prolongs the dying and diminishes both comfort and peace.

The goal of midwifery in childbirth is a healthy mother, a safe birth for mother and child, and a healthy baby. In midwifery for souls, the goal is a comfortable body, a peaceful passage, and a triumphant soul. The family's active involvement and loving presence greatly assist in the achievement of these goals.

Confusion, dissension, and any form of negativity interfere with birthing and dying, and tend to generate complications. Above all else, fear is the greatest enemy. Both birth and death take great effort, and the labor is easier to endure with eyes focused on the reward.

TWO

❦ • ❦

Family: The Basic Unit of Care

THERE ARE NOT MANY HARD and fast rules in this work, but I have identified a few from my own experiences in dealing with families. You certainly don't have to follow them, but I would like to share them with you.

Of course, patients are our top priority, but everything that happens to them takes place in the context of their family—even if they're alone.

Wounds and Battle Scars

Most patients and their families are battle-scarred by the time their journey leads them to hospice. Most cancer patients have endured some combination of surgery, chemotherapy, and radiation. Regardless of diagnosis, patients and family members alike have probably had their hopes dashed time and time again. They've had little control over their fate, and they've had their fill of hospitals and medical professionals. They are wounded, battered, and very tired.

As their hospice midwife, you are entering their lives at a vulnerable time. You must be respectful, humble, and peaceful. You may be an expert, but this is their Daddy. They know what he likes and what he doesn't like. Often, they've been doing the hands-on care for some time. Listen well to what they say and what they don't say. Take your cues from them. If they are emotionally bankrupt, you will need to step in and steer them through the immediate decisions that must be made.

Symptom control must be achieved as soon as possible. I always tell the patient and family that we are "comfort experts." Trust is quickly earned when we are able to alleviate the nausea or pain and the patient is finally comfortable, sometimes for the first time in months.

Watching a loved one suffer is excruciating, so when comfort is achieved for the patient, it is also achieved to some degree for the family. Trying to work on anything else before the patient has reached some level of comfort is futile.

The family often has many fears. You need to find ways to talk to them away from the patient. I've found it best to meet these fears head-on because what we imagine is usually worse than reality. Always look down the road a bit and help them prepare for the next step.

When family members come to trust you, they will share their worries. Often these are related to elimination. *What happens when he can't get up to go to the bathroom anymore? How will we possibly manage bedpans and, even worse, incontinence?* Many families worry about the patient's modesty, but this usually takes care of itself. As the patient approaches death there is a process of detachment; some things just don't matter anymore.

As this detachment develops, the bulk of your care is turned toward the family. They are dealing with the emotionally and physically draining task of caring for their loved one. In addition to the physical care, there's the sadness of watching their loved one deteriorate in body and detach from them in spirit. As the patient loses bodily function and interest in things that used to bring pleasure, the family loses a bit of the person they love. One man said, "I miss Dad already, and he's still here." They need a great deal of love, compassion, and encouragement from the midwife.

A Privileged Guest on the Journey

Even if you develop a beautiful relationship with the patient and family, you are still looking at a snapshot. You are seeing a moment in the life of this family. The album will grow, and you'll learn more and more about them, but you are not a member of the club.

Every family is unique, having its own set of unspoken rules, family rituals, and shared history. Sometimes not knowing what went on before is a blessing, because you only see patients as they are right now. Illness often softens people. They shed their masks and become authentic and lovable in a new way.

It's easy to be judgmental of a family, asking questions like, "How can those children turn their back on such a sweet old man during his last days?" But you don't always know the whole story.

Once we had a patient who really captured our hearts, but his family didn't seem to find him all that wonderful. He was a spunky man with a quick sense of humor, and he was so appreciative of our care. Over time, we got a picture of this man through his family's eyes. His wife said, "He never said please or thank you in his life until he got sick." His daughters dropped hints that life with Dad hadn't been ideal. Then one night, an in-law shared the story of his life with one of the nurses.

We were shocked to learn that this man had been a cruel bully, heaping physical and verbal abuse on his family right up to the day he became ill. One of the nurses who loved him most said, "I really wish I didn't know these things." In a subtle way, knowing the family history changed our regard for him. And we came to appreciate the supreme act of love it took for his family to provide his care.

I continue to be amazed at the power of family ties and the capacity for forgiveness that some families exhibit. One older alcoholic man, who had abandoned his children thirty years earlier, showed up one day on their doorstep, announced he was dying, and demanded that they care for him. And they did.

If you become a hospice midwife, you will love something in each patient—even the most unlovable. But you cannot love them as their family does.

You Are Not in Charge

God is in charge, and the family is second in command. The family has the right to make all decisions regarding their loved one's care, even bad ones. Your responsibility is seeing that family members are well informed.

It's often heartrending for the family to make the radical switch from aggressive medical care to the hospice concept of symptom control. For example, we can explain why the patient doesn't need the IV or the feeding tube anymore,* but if the family has strong objections to their removal it may be best to leave them in. Strong-arm tactics always lead to resentment and set up an adversarial relationship. The family may need to relinquish these umbilical cords gradually, and will do so if given the space.

The best way to help some families make good decisions is to allow them to make not-so-good decisions first. Pain control is an excellent example. The family may have excessive worries about over-sedation and will want to sacrifice the patient's comfort for alertness. It can be a slow process to help them realize that both comfort and alertness can usually be achieved.

Another trouble spot is when the patient moves into the active phase of dying. If the family wants to believe that the medication is causing the decreased level of con-

---

* In the active dying process, the body's systems are failing and eventually lose the ability to process or to utilize food and fluids. In this case, the patient will take in by mouth only what the body needs. Tube feedings and IV fluids strain marginally functioning systems and cause discomfort. This is not to be confused with removing food and fluids from an unconscious patient—whose body is able to utilize the nutrients—in order to cause death.

sciousness, back off of the medication until they see that this is not the case.

Sometimes what you think is a bad decision may be a good decision in disguise. Every situation is unique, and the family has to make decisions that they can live with. Although it may be hard to admit, occasionally the family is right and we are wrong!

A particularly sticky situation occurs when the patient wants one thing and the family wants another. It is your job to act as the patient's advocate.

The family may be torn between honoring the patient's wishes and seeking what they believe to be truly best for him or her. For example, the patient may insist on things that may do harm, like refusing to be turned or resisting pain medication. I had one patient who hoarded her pain medications because she had very little money and refused to let her family pay for them. This was an act of love on her part, as she tried to spare them a financial burden, but of course it caused the family great distress to see her in pain. If the patient is adamant and coherent, encourage the family to accept such desires, while working gently toward a compromise.

Loss of appetite is a frequent problem that calls for negotiation. Eating may cause discomfort to the patient, but the patient's refusal to eat causes discomfort to the family. "If he'd only eat, he'd feel better," is their lament. Food wars are common in which the family hounds the patient night and day to "eat a little something." It's the midwife's job to gently point out that comfort is our goal, and for the patient, not eating is comfort. Frequently I'll say, "At this point, food is an extra burden to the body."

Or in the case of respiratory patients, "Eating makes it more difficult to breathe."

When food has particular significance for a family—the "food equals love" school of thought—there may be nothing you can do. One family called me in the middle of the night to say, "When we put food in Grandpa's mouth, it just falls out." I've even heard of a family who tried to revive a dead man by feeding him!

The most important thing you can do is to empower the family to care for their loved one as only they can. There is something very healing in providing hands-on care. The families I've worked with who were able to assume the bulk of the patient's physical care experienced greater peace when death occurred. They had done all they could and had few, if any, regrets. And if they've been less than ideal children, even if there have been long-standing resentments, this physical care helps heal the past. It brings reconciliation and forgiveness.

This family care is more difficult to achieve in an inpatient setting. We are the nurses and the care of the patient is our job. We may feel guilty if the family does more for a patient than we do, and they in turn are often intimidated by our expertise. Whenever possible, include the family. Ask for a hand in turning, bathing, or transferring the patient to and from the bed. Encourage them to take over comfort measures, especially back rubs and mouth care. Don't intrude when they are doing something for the patient and you know a better way. Their way might well be the best, because it's done with greater love.

To be an effective midwife, you must stay on the periphery and never do for the patient what the family is willing and able to do. Praise them for their efforts, and accept them where they are. The impact you have is directly related to your gentleness and patience. Never forget that it is a singular blessing to be allowed into a family at such an intimate moment. And don't forget to pray.

You Can't Fix Sick Families

When family members have nursed hurts for years you can't expect them to behave themselves simply because it's the noble thing to do. Unfortunately, the anticipatory grief of losing a loved one often magnifies the problems in a family instead of pulling them together. If a family has a history of dealing with crises by running away, lashing out, or scapegoating, that is probably how they will react this time.

Divorce and remarriage often complicate the picture in a troubled family. Nothing is more distressing to me than when a family tries to exclude certain members from visiting the patient because of their own animosities. One particularly afflicted family turned Grandma's last days into a spirited game of "capture the flag." They loved Grandma almost as much as they despised each other. As if to demonstrate this, they kidnapped her from each other's homes. I suppose the family member's home she finally died in was the winner. So what are you going to do with a family like that? Love them the best you can.

All families with difficulties will tug on the midwife's heart, but the most challenging situations occur when a family member, or patient, reminds us of a difficult person in our own lives. When that happens, be on your guard to keep from responding in a personal way. One hospice midwife I know has a rocky relationship with her mother, who tries to control her life. She has to be particularly cautious when dealing with controlling mothers in her work. There may even be times when you need to step aside and let someone else take over.

I asked one hospice midwife how she deals with difficult families. She said, "It takes the absolute anointing of the Holy Spirit." Don't ever underestimate the power of prayer and the extraordinary graces that surround the dying.

...But God Can

I learned this lesson when I received a call one night from a hysterical family member, insisting that I come out right away. Her mother had been admitted to the hospice program that afternoon but had died at home a few hours later. The woman was sobbing so hard I could barely understand her, but I finally put it together. She was calling from a convenience store. I could hear the other family members running up and down the aisles, sobbing and shrieking. No one was willing to stay in the same house with a dead woman. When I asked if they were all there in the store, she sobbed, "No, some of them are outside running around the gas pumps."

I told her I'd be there as soon as I could, but I knew that it would be at least twenty minutes. I jumped in the car, driving like a maniac and all the while begging the Lord to send his peace to that family. When I arrived at the convenience store, there was no one there, so I drove to their house. With much trepidation I went inside, fearing that the silence meant they'd committed mass suicide. But there they all were, sitting around their dead mother's bed, as peaceful and calm as could be. Now that's a miracle!

Sometimes the healing is gradual. A colleague shared a story about a patient who spent her whole life manipulating her children. Her daughter was a busy young mother, but she opened her home to the woman and provided for her care. Predictably, this patient was difficult to care for. Even though her symptoms were controlled, her spiritual pain was extreme. She demanded a physical healing from God and would settle for nothing less. She had no peace; nor would she let anyone within ten miles of her have peace either, if she could help it. One day, her daughter met the midwife at the door and screamed, "I can't stand it anymore! I hate her!"

As the patient's condition deteriorated, however, a change took place. She no longer had the upper hand; the roles gradually reversed. When death was approaching, the daughter told the midwife, "She's not in control anymore! She's going to die, and there's not a thing in the world she can do about it." The daughter took excellent care of her mother, and by the time death occurred, great healing had taken place.

THREE

✦

The Work of Dying

WHEN A PATIENT IS ADMITTED to hospice in the early labor stage, the first priority is to control symptoms. Then you have some space for building a relationship. Now, this is a paradox. The work of the dying is to detach from the people and things of this world, and here you are trying to attach. But you are acting as a guide for the journey, and the patient can sense that.

One hospice midwife spent two hours listening as a family described their father's abusive behavior toward his nurses. When they felt she was adequately prepared they cautiously led her in to meet the patient, who had not been told she was coming. He took her hand, grinned, and exclaimed, "I've been waiting for you!"

A hospice midwife can be a breath of fresh air for the patient and family. And hospice care at its best dispels the stale energy of chronic sadness. Humor has served me well in this early stage! Many times I have walked into a patient's room and said, "It's your lucky day, because I'm your nurse. Rub my belly and I'll give you three wishes." There's nothing that brings people together faster than laughter, and it's often been in short supply for too long.

Touch is a universal language that can help develop a relationship. It's also healing, so don't be afraid. If patients seem to be especially reserved, test the waters with a pat on the arm or a squeeze of the hand. The worst thing that can happen is they'll jerk away or ask you to stop.

The Urgency to Love

With terminally ill patients, there is an urgency to love quickly if you're going to love at all. Be generous and openly affectionate. Patients often feel ugly because of the toll illness has taken on the body. Hugs and kisses send a message that they are still lovable.

When I first meet a patient, I always ask, "Have you been sick a long time?" There is a need to tell the history of the terminal illness in the same way that any traumatic event must be told time and time again. And if you are going to accompany this person on a journey, it's important that you understand the terrible twist of events that have brought you into the situation.

When the symptoms are controlled and some really good days are experienced, patients may declare that they're recovering, and the family may share this delusion. Whenever patients tell me that they are better, or that a healing has taken place, I rejoice with them. I say, "It's wonderful that you're feeling so well. This is a gift, whether it lasts a day or a lifetime. Enjoy it!" Denial is a powerful defense mechanism, and it isn't bad. It's just a defense. We all defend ourselves the best way we can, and if the patient is denying the approaching death, leave it alone. Never lie, but don't tell people more than they want to hear. There is no need to crush a hurting person with the full weight of the truth.

Life Review

Slowly, as you share experiences and earn trust by "wasting time" together, the patient will begin to open up to you. An important work of the dying is life review, sorting out the events of life and finding meaning. This usually comes in fits and spells, so always be eager to listen to stories. They're new to you, so you can often generate more inter-est and enthusiasm than the family, who may have heard them many times.

When the pathology works very quickly, or when the diagnosis is not made until the very end, patients and fam-ilies are rushed to complete their emotional and spiritual business. They especially need a guide because they may not know where their attention should be focused. The midwife's ability to guide is directly related to her willing-ness to be a channel of grace. One midwife told me the story of a distraught family who clung to the bedside of their unresponsive mother one Christmas day. This mid-wife felt inspired to ask them if they wanted to move their mother, bed and all, into the living room by the Christmas tree. They agreed, and soon they had placed their mother's bed directly in front of the tree.

Then an amazing thing happened. The woman woke up. The midwife asked if there was anything she wanted. She said, "Yes. A cigarette and a glass of wine would be nice." They rolled the head of her bed up and she took one puff from the cigarette and a couple sips of wine. Then she shared some things about her life that her family had never heard before. When she finished, she looked at her son and said, "It's time now." And she died. The midwife's willingness to act on an inspiration allowed that woman to share with her children a final act of love.

Life review, however, usually takes weeks or even months. Suggest bringing out photo albums to stimulate the process. If the family asks about calling out-of-town relatives, tell them to do it at once. Encourage the family members to come and spend time while the patient is still able to visit, and to say the things that need to be said.

Reconciliation

Look for chances to spend time alone with patients, who may need to say things to you that they can't comfortably share with the family. Often there is lack of forgiveness in some area, and this must be resolved for a peaceful death to take place. If the death is approaching quickly, you may have to be a little pushy in encouraging the patient and family to forgive while there's time. If it's not possible for them to do this in person, encourage letter writing.

I suggest listening with compassion to stories of past hurts, and then gently asking, "But does it really matter now?" If they're Christians, call attention to the Lord's

Prayer: "Forgive us our trespasses, as we forgive those who trespass against us." Remind people that forgiveness isn't a feeling but an act of the will.

Am I Going to Die?

Patients may choose to talk with you about things the family won't let them say, especially about their approaching death. I believe that every patient will talk about death eventually. If you are the person they share with, you are blessed. But it won't happen unless you listen with your heart. I've noticed that patients often make oblique references to dying just to test the waters. Don't ever let an opportunity to listen pass. Even if they change the subject, you've established an unspoken agreement that it's okay to talk about this when they're ready.

Occasionally, patients ask me, "Am I going to die?" That question always leaves a lump in my throat, and I try to remember to pray first before responding. You must be honest, but the wording of your response must be finely tuned to the patient's need. You may very well say the wrong thing, but if you roll with the punches and let the patient set you straight, you'll probably be forgiven.

When patients broach the subject, I ask, "Are you afraid?" or "What is the worst thing that could happen?" (Some men, especially young ones, will be offended if you ask about fear, but naming it is half the battle.) Try to zone in on the specifics. The number-one fear is for the well-being of their families after they die, and a close second is fear of the actual death. *Will it hurt? Will it be awful for my family to see? Will I die choking or gasping for air?* Some patients worry that they'll die suddenly, before they're ready.

Most people haven't seen anyone die, or their only experience of death is what they've heard or seen on TV. I reassure them that death is usually a very gentle, gradual process. Even though I know it can happen, I tell them I've never seen anyone choke to death, which is true. I tell them that we will do everything within our power to see that they don't hurt. And I describe the physical process if they want to know.

Then I ask, "What do you think will happen after you die?" Most patients have given this a lot of thought and candidly share their beliefs with me. But occasionally a patient will say, "I just don't know." My next question is, "Do you believe in God?" If they say no, I retreat and storm heaven with prayers. But when they say that they do believe in God, I share what I've seen with my own eyes.

I tell them about patients who saw angels and loved ones already on the other side. I tell them about patients who die with an expression of radiant joy, who obviously are seeing something beautiful at the moment of death. And then, with their permission, I pray with them.

Spiritual Distress

I have read over and over that hospice staff should never try to obtain a last-minute conversion, that we should just accept the patients where they are. "People die the way they live," seems to be the motto. I agree that there is no place for proselytizing in this work, but each patient has a body and a soul, and the soul is more important by far.

A co-worker had a patient who was in deep spiritual distress, evidenced by extreme fear and restlessness unrelated to physical symptoms, and she asked me to go see him. "He's an atheist," she said, "so you can't pray with him." My answer was, "Of course I can, but he doesn't have to know about it."

I had called on my informal community of prayer warriors upon hearing of his distress, so he'd been steeped in prayer for almost twenty-four hours when I finally went to visit him. His distress was markedly improved when I arrived, and I prayed silently at his bedside as he slept.

I gently touched his wrist to take his pulse, and he stirred slightly. I whispered, "It's okay. I'm Kathy, from hospice." He opened his eyes and looked into my eyes so deeply, I felt he could see into my soul. It seemed to me that he knew why I was there. I never spoke to him about God, because I felt it would be insensitive to do so in front of his profoundly atheistic family. But there was no need; I ministered to him just the same.

On the other end of the spectrum, I'll share a story with you from a courageous, free-spirited midwife whose faith and hospice vocation were both quite new. She admitted a spiritually distressed patient to hospice at the point of death, and asked the family about the woman's faith. They replied that she had none, and neither did they.

Now, God would have had to send me a personalized telegram to persuade me to do this, but my friend asked if she could pray with the woman. The family quickly answered no, so she asked if she could pray silently at the bedside! They consulted a bit, and hesitantly agreed. The midwife related that her silent prayer was along these lines: "God, I don't know this person, but she seems like a nice enough lady. Surely you won't let her die without any faith in you!" She popped in and out of the room, silently praying each time.

At first, the family watched her suspiciously, but after two hours of this the midwife found the family gathered around the woman, confidently urging her to trust in God and go to him. She died soon after that—a peaceful death. Amazing grace!

It has been said that there are no atheists in foxholes. The dying process is the ultimate foxhole for those with little or no faith. The few patients I've had who claimed to be atheists changed their "no" to a "maybe" toward the end. They want to believe in a loving and forgiving God, and as a Christian midwife for souls it would be irresponsible not to gently share my faith with them when presented with the opportunity.

Once we had an extremely troubled young man at the in-patient hospice. From his family's account, he had squandered his life and left a trail of hurt in his wake. He never slept, but constantly thrashed in his bed and refused our attempts to comfort him. After medicating him aggressively for days, we came to the conclusion that he suffered from tremendous spiritual pain.

One evening we decided to use the "tag-team" prayer approach. We took turns sitting in his room in silent prayer. I had the second shift, and after about thirty minutes he looked at me and I saw something in his eyes that gave me the green light. I asked if he was afraid, and he snarled, "No!" and pretended to go to sleep.

I continued to pray, and a little later he said, "Of course I'm afraid! Who wouldn't be?" I asked, "What part scares you the most?" He said, "The whole damn thing," and pretended to sleep again.

Then he turned and looked at me and I asked if he believed in God. He said yes, so I said, "He's a forgiving God, and he loves you more than you love yourself. All you have to do is ask for his forgiveness."

He pretended to sleep again, and I continued to pray. Finally, in the voice of a small, frightened child he said, "I would ask for forgiveness, but I don't know how."

"Then you're in luck," I said, "because I do. I'll go first, and you can repeat the words." We prayed the most beautiful prayer, and I can assure you it didn't come from me. When we finished, he closed his eyes and slept for the first time in a week.

I wasn't there when he died, but they told me he saw angels.

FOUR

≈ • ≈

Signs of Active Labor

Dying Is a Physical Process

THERE ARE DEFINITE PHYSICAL SIGNS that signal the beginning of the active dying phase. They may appear one by one over a period of days or weeks, or they may come on all at once over a few hours. You may not see all of them, but you will see some combination of these signs. Remember, dying is a process.

First you'll see increasing weakness, beginning in the legs. The patient will lose the ability to walk without assistance, then to bear weight while standing, and finally to change position in bed. The patient will then need to be turned every two or three hours to provide comfort and prevent bedsores. The voice will also become weaker, and the patient will spend more and more time sleeping.

You will also notice increasing difficulty in swallowing. Offer soft foods, and then change to thickened liquids only. As the physical condition deteriorates, the patient will only be able to take a few sips with a syringe or a teaspoon of flavored ice. When even sips cause choking, just moisten the mouth with water or artificial saliva. If the patient is able to talk at this point, I ask if he or she wants water; it's helpful for the family to hear from the patient that he or she is not suffering from thirst.

The patient's general appearance begins to change. The knees, lower legs, and sometimes the arms develop reddish-purple splotches, called mottling. There may be cyanosis (a bluish discoloration of the skin due to lack of oxygen in the blood) of the feet, hands, and lips. The neck hyperextends, sometimes to such a degree that only the crown of the head touches the mattress when you remove the pillow. The earlobes and ears relax until the entire ear lays flat against the head. You will also notice coldness over bony prominences, especially the knees, elbows and nose. In the final hours before death, the mandible, or jawbone, will become cold, and the skin may take on a waxy appearance.

As the body loses its ability to regulate temperature, the patient may be feverish one minute and cool the next. Sometimes the fever stays up (a terminal fever), and nothing will bring it down. I give aspirin or Tylenol suppositories every four hours just in case the fever causes discomfort, but I do not check the temperature with a thermometer. There's no need to gather this information if nothing can be done about it, and knowing that the temperature is 104 only makes the family anxious. Even though we were taught in nursing school to use ice packs under the arms to bring down a fever, ice is not comforting and should never be placed on the body of a dying person.

There is usually a period of restlessness, lasting from a few hours to a few days. Avoiding falls can be a major undertaking. At home, if there isn't a hospital bed, you can sometimes use heavy furniture as a barrier, or put the bed down on the floor. If at all possible, use chemical restraints instead of physical ones.

As the kidneys shut down, urinary output diminishes; the urine turns a dark color. Often, the lungs become congested. Usually there are gaps in the breathing pattern, called apnea; the patient can take as long as forty-five seconds to take another breath. Even though oxygen doesn't seem to make much difference at this point, families often request it. It certainly doesn't cause any harm.

Pharyngeal rales, sometimes called the "death rattle" by families, don't seem to have as much to do with fluid in the lungs as with the total relaxation of the body. When the cough reflex is diminished or lost, even a small amount of phlegm vibrating against relaxed vocal cords makes a terrible gurgle. I always tell the family that the patients don't seem bothered by this, but listening to it is torture. They may beg you to suction, but this is usually futile as well as traumatic. The best approach is medication to dry up the secretions. Sometimes repositioning the patient will diminish the rattle. If you find a position in which the sound is less noticeable, leave the patient there until the medication has a chance to work.

It's helpful to explain to the family that the body is focusing on keeping the brain, heart, and lungs going, and sacrifices other functions since the reserves are so limited. When digestion presents too great a strain, the patient loses all appetite. When the kidneys can no longer function, the ability to swallow fluids vanishes. Tube feedings, IVs, suction machines and the like cause more harm than good. Above all, these measures rob the patient of peace.

These changes should never come as a surprise to the family. Prepare them ahead of time, providing bits of information here and there as opportunities arise.

Dying Is a Spiritual Process

There are also spiritual signs that death is approaching. You will see a gradual detachment from material things. Many patients lose interest in all forms of amusement, such as TV and music. They have little tolerance for conversation, and even the most outgoing persons begin to prefer silence. Things that had exaggerated importance before, such as appearance or modesty, are abandoned. The spiritual work is too strenuous, the journey too difficult to carry excess baggage.

The final detachment is from relationships. The patient may push away loved ones whom they clung to only a short time before. When one patient would no longer let his beloved dog sit beside his chair, I told the family he was getting close. He died three days later.

I always explain that the family must not mistake this detachment for lack of love. It's an early leave-taking in preparation for the final one. Patients simply can't focus on where they're going until they've distanced themselves a little from all the people they leave behind.

Many patients will talk about seeing dead relatives. One man said of his dead brother, "Tell Bill to come in. He just stays out there in the hall." Another said, "My brother-in-law came to see me last night, and he's been dead for years. He just stood there and looked at me, and then he was gone." I've never heard of a patient being frightened by this.

There is usually a period of spiritual restlessness, which corresponds to the transition stage of childbirth when many women experience a moment of despair. They lose hope that they can birth this child and want to escape from the labor.

Even though there are physical reasons for this restlessness, like hypoxia (a deficiency of oxygen reaching body tissues) and kidney failure, I believe that it's primarily a sign of intense struggle between the will and the spirit. And I've noticed that it is more severe and prolonged for patients who are alienated from God.

Patients may try to get out of bed, take off their clothes, and generally thrash about. If they have been extremely dependent on oxygen they may take it off. They will not listen to reason and will often insist that they must get out of bed to do some form of work.

This stage can be very disturbing to the family, because the patients may get angry for not letting them out of the bed. I reassure families that it normally lasts twelve to twenty-four hours, and when it passes the patient is usually more peaceful and resigned than before. This is sometimes called "pre-death restlessness," because death usually follows within a few hours or days. Often, it is the first sign of the active dying phase.

Sometimes there's a period of confusion that may be an actual reliving of life experiences. There's no way to know for sure, but some patients' life review seems to be really experienced instead of shared in stories. I've seen men drive teams of horses and carry out a wide variety of physical labor from their hospital beds, while women usually care for children and cook elaborate dinners. One woman experienced a series of disasters for two solid weeks, everything from floods to tornadoes, and spent every waking hour rendering aid to victims.

A seasoned hospice midwife told me to ask patients to tell me their age when I see this, especially if they no longer recognize their children. She says it's been very comforting to families, in her experience, to explain that Mother doesn't recognize them because in her mind they haven't been born yet. Once this important work of life review is accomplished, patients often return to the present and respond appropriately.

As the time of death approaches the patient ascends to a higher spiritual plane. We talk of decreased level of consciousness, but what really happens is an increased level of consciousness. The best way to understand this is to see the dying process as a journey; the final stage is crossing a bridge. As patients move closer to the other side, they can see where they're going while still maintaining an awareness of the people around them.

"An Angel from Heaven Appeared..."

When patients travel far enough to get a glimpse of the other side, they begin to stare at the point where the wall and ceiling meet. I call this "watching the angel show." Their eyes travel back and forth, stopping at one point and then another when something particularly captures their interest. When the family speaks, they briefly make eye contact, then return their attention to the ceiling, as if they prefer the company of the unseen guests.

Sometimes patients talk. You'll see their lips move, then they'll pause and wrinkle their brow in a listening pose, and then the lips will move again, but the words are often inaudible. I've occasionally seen patients alternate between talking out loud to the family and silently to the unseen guests. It's as if the volume on their voice is turned off when they talk to their friends on the ceiling.

Even when patients can still talk at this point they usually can't put into words what they're experiencing. I always ask anyway, because it's a great blessing for the families—and the midwife—to see a little of the other side through their eyes. More than once, I've heard patients announce joyfully, "There are angels all over this room!" One lady said, "Why didn't you tell me it would be so beautiful?" I said, "Because I haven't been down that road." She laughed and said, "Oh, that's right," and turned her attention back to the angel show.

When the patient can't talk, I point out to the family the movement of eyes and lips. I wave my hand in front of the patient's face, and when the patient doesn't blink I say, "She's seeing things we can't see." I share stories of patients who tried to explain it to me, which is usually a great source of peace for the family. I always try to turn their eyes to the other side, too, to help them focus on where their loved one is going instead of on the deterioration of the body, which can be distressing, even frightening at times.

A Time for Detachment

Because this is a time of detachment from the body, avoid any unnecessary or vigorous movement of the patient. I imagine a woman at the point of childbirth, and how she can't bear to be handled or bothered. Repositioning must be done for comfort, but ever so gently. At this point, it's enough to alternate pressure points by placing or removing pillows and raising or lowering the head of the bed every few hours. Assuming that the patient's pain is controlled, the three things that bring comfort at this stage are artificial tears when the eyes are open constantly, artificial saliva spray or drops of water to keep the mouth moist, and prayer. Lots of prayer.

Once the restlessness has passed, I put down the side-rails if the patient is in a hospital bed. This is a symbolic way to drop barriers, and the family often takes this cue to move closer to the patient. You are the guide. If you speak softly and touch gently, chances are the family will do the same. This is the time when families who've resisted forgiveness or open acknowledgments of love will sometimes say the things that need to be said.

Your job will be more difficult if the patient is already in the active stage at your first contact. Get to know what kind of person he or she is from the family. Even though you never had a chance to ease into the relationship, you can still connect with the patient, as well as the family, through peaceful presence and silent prayer.

FIVE

≻ • ≺

Praying Them over the Wall

Soul-to-Soul Time

EVEN WITH COMPLICATION-FREE DEATHS, I believe that many patients benefit from a gentle nudge to make the leap to the other side. I think of this nudge as "praying them over." There has been slow detachment throughout the labor, but at the end there must be complete abandonment. I am convinced that prayer greatly aids the patient in this final effort. At this stage, it's best to follow the monastic advice, "Speak only when your words will improve on silence."

Occasionally the patient will begin to moan at the end. First, look for clues that this is a result of pain. Does the moaning increase when the patient is moved? Does it diminish after breakthrough pain medicine is given? When I am convinced that the patient's pain is controlled, I call this the moaning of the soul. As Saint Paul explains in Romans 8:26, "when we do not know how to pray properly, then the Spirit personally makes our petitions for us in groans that cannot be put into words."

A Time of Ultimate Choice

This is a time of choice, the ultimate choice—for God or against God. Patients who have lived as friends of God make this choice by second nature. Those who have lived alienated from him have a much harder time.

I have seen things that convince me that at least some patients are tempted to despair at the hour of death. Many times I have seen patients arguing at the end. Some say, "No," over and over with each breath. I always thought they were saying no to death. Then a family told me their father looked like he was defending his faith, which he had done often in his life. I wondered about this for a long time, and then I was blessed with a patient who talked to me throughout this battle.

This woman was a dear, and I had taken care of her for several weeks. She faced her death with peaceful acceptance and deep faith. On the morning she died she began to watch the angel show. I was sitting beside her, feeling very peaceful, when her expression changed and she was overcome with fear.

"Get him out of here!" she demanded, pointing to the corner of the room. I asked whom she meant, and she said, "That mean man! He's ugly and he's dark, and he says I can't have my place!" I asked if she meant her place in heaven, and she said yes. I told her that she belonged to Jesus and no one could take her place. "That's right!" she said, and began to argue silently and shake her finger at the corner of the room.

I stayed with her in silent prayer and she became peaceful again, only to startle every few minutes and cry for me to make the mean man leave. This went on for about two hours, and then she asked to sit up. Her children supported her back as she stared at the ceiling, and her face radiated peace. She turned to me and asked, "Is that mean man still here?" I asked her if she saw him, and she searched the ceiling before answering no. I said, "Go to your place. Jesus is waiting for you." And she did.

That experience was a great gift to me. Sometimes I'm tempted to slack off from prayer when a patient seems to be in good shape spiritually, and then I remember that woman. Prayer is food, comfort, and strength for the dying.

Complications in the Dying Process

As a midwife, your job at the end of the journey is to keep your spiritual antenna out for signs of trouble along the way. The patient is usually unable to talk at this point, so look into his or her eyes. The eyes are the window to the soul.

Fear

If you see fear, you must intervene. Speak directly into the patient's ear and talk very softly of the love and forgiveness of God. I always call on the Holy Spirit so the message is individualized, but I'll share a sample with you.

"God loves you so very much, and he wants you with him forever. Don't worry about your family; God will take care of them. Trust him. Fear doesn't come from God. Just keep your eyes on that beautiful light. You will not die. Your soul will live forever. Just lay down your body. You don't need it anymore. Go to the light."

After a short coaching session, I settle in at the bedside and pray silently. When I feel the need I speak; otherwise I try to provide a peaceful, prayerful presence. I've seen beautiful results from this method, but don't get discouraged if the fear continues.

Sometimes it comes and goes, and sometimes it lasts for days regardless of your efforts. Remember, this is not your journey. You may have a clue, but there's no way of knowing what the patient is struggling with or experiencing. You can only do your best and then trust God with the rest.

Once I had a patient who was terrified of God's judgment. We talked of this at length over the course of his illness, and called his minister out numerous times at his request. Toward the end, he tried repeatedly to make a confession to one of the nurses, but each time he fell asleep before he got to the heart of it.

When he reached the active stage, his restlessness was unbelievable. We gave him massive doses of medication with little effect. This went on for days, and no amount of prayer or coaching seemed to help.

One night, when his body seemed pushed to the absolute limit, I whispered in his ear, "Do you see the light?" He nodded his head. "Go to the light," I said. "You've asked God's forgiveness. Now it's time to trust him. Go to the light." Even though he hadn't spoken in two days, his voice rang out clearly, "Don't rush me." He lived two more weeks.

Permission

When the patient seems peaceful and all the physical signs are present, prolonged dying may be caused in part by the family's refusal to let go. Sometimes this is obvious. One woman quit breathing and seemed dead numerous times, but the family stroked her all over and called her name, crying loudly, and she would pick up and begin to breathe again. This went on until they were completely exhausted, and they finally released her.

One woman who had nursed her husband through years of illness followed our advice and gave her permission. But she sounded like an athletic coach, saying over and over, "You can do it, I'm not going to let you stop until you get there, you're almost there, keep going...." Of course, her true message was, "Keep fighting."

I tried to guide the woman by gently urging the patient to abandonment, but she did not take my clues. Even though this was no help at all to the patient, I didn't interfere, because it was a necessary part of the woman's journey. Eventually she wore herself out and gave real permission.

Sometimes lack of permission is not so obvious. When I was a new hospice nurse we had a patient who was ready to die; the family appeared quite reconciled to his death, but he seemed to have hit a brick wall. An experienced nurse said, "I don't know who it is, but somebody is holding back the Holy Spirit."

Since then, I can't count the times I've seen a family member, often the wife, say all the right things but the patient lived on and on. Finally, she says, "I can't stand to see him this way anymore. I want it to be over." And that's the day the patient dies.

Sometimes it's the patient who won't let go of the family. One ninety-two-year-old woman pulled back from the brink of death time and time again. Finally she confided to me, "I can't go; my girls need me!" Her "girls" were pushing seventy. After they reassured her that they'd be okay, she died within hours.

Children especially need the approval of their parents to die. When permission is withheld, the patient will finally die, but many times it is only when the family, or a particular family member, is out of the room.

If a patient takes an unusual amount of time to die, there is always a reason. Even if you can't figure it out, there's important work going on. That's why euthanasia is such a tragedy, aside from the fact that it's murder. It robs the patient, and the family, of the time they need to resolve vital issues, even if they can't see any purpose to the delay.

Depending on Miracles

Occasionally families with deep faith will insist that a miraculous healing will take place. Do not contradict them. Miracles can and do happen.

After I've gained their trust, I ask if I can pray with them. I then say, "Jesus, you are the divine physician. Please heal _____ in body, mind, and spirit, according to your will. And please give him and his loving family the grace to accept your will, whatever it may be."

These families usually have a very difficult time with the death. Call in their pastor, minister, or hospice pastoral care staff when you think the end is near.

Near "Bad Death" Experiences

Nothing is more frightening than to see a patient at the point of death in terrible spiritual shape. Even if the patient is verbally unresponsive, you know this person is in trouble when you see severe agitation that doesn't respond to medication. Occasionally, there's also a distinct sense of evil. When this happens, you enter true spiritual warfare, and it takes everything you've got. Always request pastoral assistance.

The strangest experience I ever had with a spiritual crisis involved a woman who seemed well grounded in her faith. I had taken care of her for three nights in a row, and we had prayed together minutes before she had a sudden cardiac death.

I held her hand and prayed, and then I heard a little agonal breath two or three minutes after I thought she was gone. The breaths got deeper and came closer together. Suddenly her eyes flew open and she said in a guttural voice, "I don't want to die." I will never forget those eyes. They were brimming with hate. I prayed out loud for her, and every time I mentioned the name of Jesus, her eyes flashed hatred. She began to swing her arm at me, trying to make me stop praying. I blessed her with holy water, a sign of the waters of Baptism, and continued to pray. Eventually the hate left her eyes, and when she spoke again her voice was back to normal. "Please help me, I don't want to die," she whispered.

Her family arrived about that time and asked that we call her priest. Of course, I should have already called him, but it's hard to think in such an emotionally charged situation. After the priest prayed with her she was completely back to normal. Twenty-four hours later she died peacefully.

Occasionally I hear stories from hospice midwives about bad deaths. Basically they are like the "near bad deaths" I've described, only the patient never clearly pulled out of the agitated state. They happen very infrequently, and I have not yet been present for one, thank God.

The Request for Death

In my experience, patients who struggle with suicidal feelings are usually suffering from uncontrolled pain or other distressing symptoms, coupled with a sense of being burdensome or unloved. It's not uncommon for the midwife to hear requests for suicide assistance on the first encounter with patients. But once the symptoms are controlled to some degree, and we have a chance to love them well, they can usually get on with the business of living.

Another spot in the journey when suicide might be mentioned is the stage that corresponds to transition in childbirth. The hospice midwife must be an especially sensitive guide and "labor coach" if this occurs.

I have seen laboring women, almost at the point of delivery, insist that they must get their purse and go home and perhaps resume this unpleasant business on a better day. No labor nurse in her right mind would call that woman a cab, and no hospice midwife worth her salt would ever condone a patient's suicidal wish.

I'm hearing more and more about patients planning suicide as a way to control their death, and they present it as a peaceful and dignified exit. There is nothing peaceful or dignified about murder, and it is the midwife's responsibility to do everything in her power to dissuade them. As always, pray that you may be a channel of grace, and you'll be given the words.

When a patient brings up suicide, try to explore the reasons the patient wants to commit suicide, and offer reassurance and comfort. I tell the patient that together we can learn to focus on the living instead of the dying and continue to grow to the very end. No trap doors, no cheating.

If you're present for an apparently bad death, or if your patient commits suicide, you'll need some spiritual intensive care. Even though we never know what happens between a soul and God at the moment of death, when someone dies in obvious distress you're bound to wonder if you could have done more. There may have been a time you had the opportunity to speak to that patient about God and didn't. There may have been subtle signs of suicidal thoughts that you didn't pick up on. Learn from your mistakes, forgive yourself, and go on.

One of the few bad deaths I've heard of happened in the presence of a midwife who was a powerful pray-er, and the patient died cursing God. Remember, this is not your journey. Each soul must make the choice alone. Above all, trust in the unfathomable mercy of God and ask him to fill you again with his peace.

SIX

❦ • ❦

Timing

THE INEVITABLE QUESTION FROM the family is, "How much longer?" First, you must look at the course of the illness. Have there been small declines and plateaus, or are you seeing a nosedive over a period of a few days? Usually, as the illness goes, so goes the dying.

Death of the Young

There are two situations that defy even an educated guess regarding time of death. The first is death of the young. By young, I mean forty years or younger. The younger the patient, the more difficult the death for all involved.

Young people aren't supposed to die. People in their teens and twenties seem to fight hardest and deny longest. I've often noticed that they won't lie down. No matter how exhausted they are, they want to sit up. They insist on walking even when you'd think it was impossible.

With such strong hearts and wills, these patients often live much longer than expected. They continue to fight for the sake of their families and may feel that by dying they will fail their loved ones.

Encourage the loved ones of young patients to tell them how heroic their fight has been and how proud they are. Give permission to let go. When the patient finally reaches the stage of abandonment, death follows quickly—sometimes within hours or even minutes.

Sudden Death Experience

The other situation that's hard to anticipate is sudden death. A common cause of sudden death in cancer patients is massive hemorrhage. If the bleeding is internal, the signs are an abrupt decline in condition; clammy, pale skin; and a rapid, thready pulse. Usually the patient is afraid, and so is the family. Medicate the patient's anxiety and pain, and administer oxygen if the patient has trouble breathing. Stay calm, speak softly, and pray hard. Death usually comes very quickly, so gently urge the family to share their love with the patient.

Usually the bleeding is internal. If you have an idea that external bleeding might occur, prepare the family ahead of time. Tell them that it is frightening to see a lot of blood all at once, but the patient will die quickly. If the patient is at home, prearrange a crisis dose of pain medication to be given immediately. If hemorrhaging occurs, have red towels ready and instruct the family to cover the bleeding area, call the nurse/doctor, and hold the patient's hand. Fortunately, in my experience, this type of death is rare.

"A Time to Die"

Most deaths follow a predictable course. Once all the signs are present, I usually say, "From a physical standpoint, death could come at any time. If I were guessing, I'd say we're looking at seventy-two hours at the most. But I've been wrong many times." The family needs some sort of time frame, but it is very foolish to make a statement like, "She won't make it through the night."

Always point out the significance of the patient's choice in the matter. One patient told his family, "I hate to be stubborn with the Lord, but I'm just not ready to let go yet." The will to live is a powerful thing and is difficult to relinquish. A particularly strong-willed patient may defy all medical rules.

When patients are being "stubborn with the Lord" they will employ devices to stay in control at all times. They will fight sleep, fearing that if they ever really relax God will sneak up and take them. Some will doze during the day and stay up at night, when they think death is more likely to occur. I've seen patients who absolutely refused to lie down, and who slept instead in a recliner or slumped over their bedside table. One woman slept on her back with her legs bent; when she entered a deep sleep her knees would fall over and jar her awake.

An old cowboy once motioned me to his bedside and whispered, "I've got a big problem. I can see Jesus down there at the foot of my bed, and he's got his arms spread out like he wants me to come to him, but I'm just not ready to go. What should I do?"

"Just tell him the truth. He already knows. And besides, he's a gentleman. He'll wait."

The cowboy seemed satisfied. He remained calm and peaceful until his death several days later. That experience has given me the confidence to tell worried patients that God won't sneak up and take them when they're not looking. I say, "When it's your time, you'll be the first to know about it." They seem to find that comforting.

Resurrections are uncommon, but I believe that in a final illness, each person gets to choose the time of death within the limits of the human body. It's as if God waits for people to come to him by a free act of the will. I have seen four patients "resurrect." All the signs of impending death were present, but they pulled out of it for a bonus period of time ranging from two days to several months.

I once urged a Jewish woman who was very close to death to go to the light. She said, "Not today. Maybe tomorrow." Her son was present when she said that, which turned out to be a great blessing. He came to me in tears a few days later, begging me to give his mother enough morphine to "put her out of her misery."

"I can't take this anymore," he said, "it's so pointless." I reminded him of his mother's words, and told him that killing her would rob her of the time she needed to put her house in order; she just wasn't ready. He struggled to accept that. When she died the next Saturday, he told me she had always wanted to die on the Sabbath.

Another patient didn't want her death to interfere with her granddaughter's wedding. Several times each day she would ask what date it was, even when she entered the active phase of dying. The night of the wedding she was unresponsive. Someone held a phone to her ear, and her daughter told her that the wedding had been beautiful. The phone was hardly back in the cradle when the woman died.

Often patients die when continued living would mean giving up too much. I had a spunky patient who told me on several occasions that she didn't want anyone ever to wash her bottom. She maintained her independence to the end. When I found her actively dying one morning, I gently turned her over and said, "I'm just going to clean you up a bit." I could almost hear her say, "You wanna bet?" She died before I could finish.

My friend Dodie lived in horror of being bedfast and dependent. She resisted getting a hospital bed, which was a symbol of helplessness to her. We finally talked her into having the bed delivered, but she didn't spend even one night in it. The bed came at noon and she died around midnight.

Calling in the Family

An issue that may surface at this time is fear of missing the death. The family may ask you if they should call out-of-town relatives. I suggest that they be called and informed of the patient's condition. They can then make their own decision. When relatives call asking if they should fly in, I tell them to listen to their heart.

The relatives who are present become fearful of leaving. I tell them, "If you would never forgive yourself if he died without you here, then you need to stay from now on."

Then I explain my theory, which carries the weight of first-hand witness. I believe that patients will time death so that the people they want to be there will be there. Often, patients seem to wait until a minister or favorite nurse is present, perhaps so the family will be comforted during and after the death.

Some people love a crowd and will not die until every last relative is gathered in the room. Other people are very private and will wait for everyone to drift off to sleep before they go. One man, whose wife never left his side, waited for her to go to the bathroom and then slipped away.

A colleague shared with me a dramatic example of this need for privacy. She cared for a man who came within inches of death time and time again, only to pull back at the last minute. His family was very close and loving, and they desperately wanted to be with him when he died. Finally, the midwife shared her feeling that he needed to be alone. So the next time he got close they all went to the living room, but he pulled back from death again.

They finally decided, "If he wants privacy, we'll give him privacy." They all piled into the car and drove around the block. It was an extreme, loving sacrifice on their part, and he died while they were gone.

I always discuss the patient's control with the family ahead of time, trying to head guilt off at the pass. If someone is not present at the time of death, it doesn't mean they've failed or that they're loved less than the ones who are there. The patient may have believed that seeing the death would be too hard for that person. Or, perhaps the bond was so strong between them that the person's presence would have made leaving harder. Whatever the reason, remember: no one ever dies alone! Unseen friends from the other side, angels, and God himself assist the soul at the time of passage.

The Final Farewells

When death is imminent, the blood pressure drops and the heart rate increases. I rarely take blood pressures, because it's too intrusive for the patient. I do monitor the radial pulse, and I've only rarely seen death occur before the heart rate reaches 120/minute or more. The respirations become rapid and shallow, with variable periods of apnea. Sometimes there are gaps between breaths of forty-five seconds or more.

Remind the family to call in any absent family members. I always encourage them to include the children unless it looks like the death may be a difficult one. Of course, the final decision rests with the family, and you should support them in whatever they decide. Always ask the family if they want their minister called, as they may be too upset to think of it.

A few minutes before death the respirations often change abruptly. The breathing becomes very shallow, and the only movement you see is in the neck and clavicle area. This is the time to gather everyone at the bedside.

I've been a part of some beautiful good-byes. Some families sing hymns at this time; others hold hands around the bed and pray together. If they seem at a loss for what to do, I gently encourage them to tell the patient they love him, that it's okay to go, and that the family will be all right. With their permission, I lead them in prayer, ending with the Lord's Prayer. All Christians know it and can pray along, and it is a prayer of acceptance and forgiveness.

When the patient dies, I verify the fact by listening for heart and lung sounds, and I check to make sure the pupils are fixed and dilated. Sometimes death is so gentle and the last agonal respirations are spaced so far apart, it's not always clear that death has occurred. Never say, "Yes, he's gone," without a clinical assessment.

Ministering to the Bereaved

The reaction of a family to death differs from culture to culture. Some groups are noted for their emotional, demonstrative responses, seeing this as a way to honor the dead or to express love for the deceased. Other times, however, dramatic mourning is a result of guilt or despair. Regardless of the cause, your response should be silent prayer and hugs all around.

If you didn't pray at the time of death, ask the family if you can pray with them as soon as it's feasible after the initial grieving. Hold hands around the body and lead the prayer unless someone in the family wants to lead.

Always make a point of telling the family that they've done a beautiful job. And don't be afraid to cry with them.

When the time seems appropriate to do so, tidy up the body. Some families will want to leave the room while you do this, while others will want to help, or perhaps they will prefer to do it themselves. Lower the head of the bed, close the eyes, and straighten the body. Reposition the head so the mouth is not gaping open. If this is difficult to do, you can roll up a towel, pull it tight against the chin, and tuck the ends beneath the pillow. Change the diaper or padding if it's soiled. Take off the oxygen and remove or cover up any unsightly tubes. If the side-rails are up, put them down so the family can move close to say their final good-byes.

Sensitivity is needed in the immediate post-death period. The family may not be able to tell you what they want, so be attentive. Some families want time alone to linger, stroke the body, and maybe even get in the bed for a last good-bye. This can be a great source of healing.

One five-year-old boy ministered to his father in an amazing way when he was allowed to see his mother's body. When told of her death, he ran upstairs, jumped up on the bed, and looked intently into her face. "Her face is a weird color," he said. "I guess that's because she's not breathing, right?" Then he said, "And her heart's not beating either. Right?" He had a lot of questions about what the funeral home would do and what the funeral would be like.

When he asked if she'd have a glass casket like in the fairy tales, the hospice nurse thought, "Uh oh, he doesn't get it." The boy had only been told his mother was dying the day before, so there hadn't been much preparation. She gently said, "Now, when you come home from school tomorrow, your mom won't be here."

"Oh yes she will! Because I have two mothers. This one will go into the ground, but the other one is going to heaven and turn into a soul. And souls can be anywhere they want to be. They can leap tall buildings and walk through walls, and if my mom's soul wants to be with me from now on, she can." The boy and his father stayed with the body for over four hours before they were ready to call the funeral home.

I've also assisted families who couldn't bear to stay in the room after the death, and who wanted the body removed as soon as possible. When that's the case, I always volunteer to sit with the body until the funeral home personnel come. They don't always accept the offer, but those who do seem grateful that I bring it up. Support them in their wishes, and help them feel that whatever they want is the "right thing" to do.

Waiting for the funeral home personnel to come can be a difficult, awkward time. Encourage the family to tell stories about the patient. This is a lovely way to pay tribute to loved ones, to affirm their life and the impact they had on the family. When this happens, there is usually a generous amount of laughter amid the tears. I believe these preliminary "wakes" are a great source of early healing.

When it is time to carry the body out, I strongly encourage the family to leave the room. If they insist, of course I let them stay, but it is very distressing to see the dead body moved onto the stretcher. There's just no way to do it gracefully, and I've never seen a family member stay who was not upset by this.

Don't cover the face. Ask the funeral home personnel to stop if the family seems to want another good-bye in the hallway. Usually this is brief, but I've seen it take fifteen to twenty minutes. You are the family's advocate, so make sure they get all the time they need. I accompany the body to the vehicle to show my respect; sometimes the family will also come along.

Once the body is gone, I help the family gather up the patient's belongings, discreetly asking what they want to save and what they want to throw away. This can be difficult because families are so different. Some will want to keep everything, while others will seem offended that you even asked. If the death occurs at home, I remove the linens and place a blanket on the stripped bed. Seeing the bed empty can be very difficult for the family, so equipment should be removed from the house as soon as possible. Then I give a round of hugs, thank them for sharing their loved one with me, and assure them of my prayers during their bereavement.

Going to the funeral is a loving touch, although I did not do this very often when I worked for an in-patient hospice. I suppose it was self-protection. When a patient died, there was always another patient and family waiting for my attention. Some hospice nurses attend each funeral, while others only go if a close bond was formed. Whether you attend funerals or not, you need to find some way to acknowledge the death of your patients, or cumulative grief will find expression when you least expect it. One hospice nurse I know thought she was taking all those deaths in her stride, with no effect on her at all. Then she attended the funeral of her mailman, someone she'd known for a long time, but not well. As she sat in the back row, she began to weep. Her crying became loud, uncontrollable sobs, and she thought she'd never stop. Everyone at the funeral knew just how casual her relationship with the deceased had been, because she lived in a small town. She felt sure they were all thinking that there was much more to their relationship than met the eye.

SEVEN

❦ • ❧

Pastoral Care

THE INVOLVEMENT OF CLERGY and religious in this work is invaluable. They are often trained in ministry to the dying and bereaved and can be instruments of God's grace in a special way. Always try to involve them in the care of your patient as early as possible.

Working with the Family Minister

Families are often reluctant to call the pastor, especially at an inconvenient hour, because they don't want to be a bother. It's the midwife's responsibility to encourage them to call when there's a need, and to offer to make that call for them.

If a patient's religious tradition is unfamiliar to me, I learn all I can about their practices and rituals. But I don't think you need a Ph.D. in comparative religion to effectively care for patients of a different faith—as long as you act with respect and love.

In my community, almost all of my patients are Christian. But I recently served as midwife for a Buddhist couple who spoke no English. They were very spiritual, and it was beautiful to see how our love bridged the religious and language differences.

One day, when the husband's death appeared imminent, I found his wife sobbing at his bedside. We sat there for an hour with our arms around each other. I silently prayed my rosary and she whispered her prayers. We rocked back and forth, comforting each other with the comfort of God.

If the family has no ties to a church, feel them out about the involvement of the hospice staff clergy. If you have trained clergy or pastoral ministers on your staff, you and your patients are blessed. They can do such beautiful things by inching into patients' lives a bit at a time and gently ministering to their spirits.

At times it becomes apparent that the patient and family have open animosities to organized religion and clergy. In such cases, the spiritual care of the patient and family rests squarely on your shoulders. This will often take a great deal of patience on your part.

Praying for Those Who Don't Pray

I served as midwife for a man who had no interest in religion. I took care of him for eight months, and for seven of those months I didn't mention anything spiritual at all. But I loved him, listened to him, and prayed silently for him. The closest thing he'd ever had to a religious experi-

ence was reading a book titled *How to Buy Stocks.* He said
it had changed his life!

One day he became extremely short of breath and very
frightened. Since he was not receptive to touch, I just stood
by his bed in silence. He looked up at me and said, "You
don't know how much it means to me for you just to be
here." I told him I loved him, and, much to my surprise,
he said he loved me too.

It was early on a Sunday morning, and another nurse
came to take my place. I said, "I really hate to leave, but
my friend will stay here with you. I'm going to church and
I'll pray for you there."

He said, "I'd really like that," with such enthusiasm that
I gathered the courage to ask if he'd like me to pray with
him right then. He agreed. I prayed, and he closed his eyes
and went to sleep.

When I returned that evening he said, "You know, that
prayer really worked. That and the morphine." From that
point on, I'd briefly pray with him, with his permission,
whenever he had shortness of breath. This laid the
groundwork for the day when I was finally able to speak
to him about the love and forgiveness of God. I don't
think that could have happened if God hadn't given me
the patience to wait until this man was ready. He died
three days later.

Often the roles of clergy and nurse blur, and we work as
a team. But occasionally we take over spiritual care when a
pastor drops the ball. One midwife told me about a man
who came to the in-patient hospice with overwhelming
fear in his eyes. She looked at him and said, "I promise you

one thing. I will never lie to you." She had no idea why she said that at the time.

Later the man's minister came to visit, and she overheard him telling the patient that because of his sinful ways, he was going to hell and there was nothing he could do about it. Later, she found the man outside on the patio in his underwear. Now, logic would tell you that this man was confused and had wandered off, but her heart told her something else.

"Are you trying to kill yourself?" she asked, surprised by her question. He dropped his head and nodded. "It's not cold enough," she said and led him back inside to his room. Then she looked him square in the eye and said, "Can you ask for forgiveness? If you do, God will forgive you. Remember, I promised I'd never lie to you." Even though he showed no signs of impending death, the man died quite peacefully a few hours later.

Prayer with Families and Patients

It's one thing to pray in private, and quite another to pray in public. This was scary for me at first, and I know that a lot of hospice care nurses have trouble with it. You really put yourself out on a limb when you pray out loud, but if you ask the Holy Spirit, you will always be given the words. I still find it helpful to memorize prayers for the time of death, then tailor them for particular families.

Before, I felt my silent prayers were sufficient. But since I've begun praying out loud with patients, I see the fruits. It really helps to remind them of the goodness and forgiveness of God, of his deep love for them and his constant presence.

I often pray with patients in times of distress or as a closure to a visit when it feels right. I always ask permission first and have never been turned down. In fact, most people really appreciate it and find it touching.

You can also use this for the benefit of those who care for the patient. For instance, ask God to grant the patient love if he's snappy, patience if he's demanding, or a clear mind if he's asking the same questions over and over.

Just plunge in, and don't be afraid. Perfect love casts out fear, and we are in the service of Perfect Love.

EIGHT

❦ • ❧

Spiritual Exercises for the Midwife

PROFESSIONAL ATHLETES SPEND HOURS each day exercising their bodies. The hospice midwife is a spiritual athlete. You must exercise and nourish your soul daily, or you won't have the stamina and grace you need to accompany others on their journey to God. There's no magic formula, but I can share what works for me and other midwives I know.

(Let it be known that I am radically, joyfully, one-hundred-percent Roman Catholic. Please don't take the zeal I have for my faith as disrespect for yours.)

Become a Pray-er

Set aside time each morning and evening for conversation with God. How can you share God with others if you're not even on speaking terms with him? Since prayer is food for the journey, you need several kinds to nourish you throughout the day.

Community Prayer

Don't neglect worship on the Sabbath. We are the Body of Christ, and we need the prayers and support of our community.

Daily Mass is the center of my day, and I find it a great source of grace. I've also found that gathering together with my co-workers for prayer before rounds makes a startling difference in the way the day goes. If we're rushed for time, we just join hands and pray: "Lord, grant us prayerful spirits, joyful hearts, gentle hands, strong backs, and the help of your angels to do your work this day."

If your co-workers aren't like-minded, you'll need to find support elsewhere from kindred spirits who can share your joys and sorrows. A loving spiritual community, organized or informal according to your needs, is essential for the nurturing of this vocation. We have all been given a variety of gifts. Brothers and sisters who act as silent prayer warriors are invaluable in this work.

I believe that our friends who are in heaven are attentive and enthusiastic pray-ers. If we pray for each other on earth, why would we stop praying because we've crossed the finish line? I frequently call on Mary, the Mother of God, and various saints I'm fond of, as well as relatives, friends, and former patients. Love, by its nature, is generous and never-ending. I feel the perfected love of my friends in heaven, and I know they assist me in my work.

Scriptural Prayer

Get up a little earlier each morning and pray with the Bible. Just read slowly until something grabs your heart, then savor it.

Many find the psalms to be a particularly nourishing form of prayer. An excellent way to pray them is through the Liturgy of the Hours. This form of prayer goes back to the first century and is prayed daily by most priests and religious as well as many lay people. When you pray the morning or evening Office, you are joining your prayers with millions of Christians around the world.

Prayers of Petition

Prayers of petition are very important, but all too often they are our only form of prayer. I call them "begging" prayers. Present God with the needs of your family, patients, co-workers, and all those commended to you.

I try to let my prayers be universal. For instance, I pray, "Please help my patient, Mary, to trust in God's mercy, as well as all those who are tempted to despair this day." Get as much mileage as you can from each prayer! There are so few of us who pray today, so we must pray as if we were many.

Then pray for yourself. Invite the Holy Spirit to dwell within you. "The fruit of the Spirit is love, joy, peace, patience, kindness, goodness, faithfulness, gentleness, self-control" (Gal 5:22–23).

Pray for an increased trust in God, which leads to fear-lessness in the face of death. If you carry fear within you, it will only add to the patient's distress.

Last but not least, pray for the virtue of humility. Pride is the enemy of the spiritual life. It leads you to rely on yourself, which will be your downfall in this work. Never forget that you are merely an instrument of God's love for your patient.

Prayers of Praise and Thanksgiving

Such prayers keep us from feeling like such beggars; they also remind us of the countless beautiful gifts we've received.

Lifting Your Heart to God

For centuries Christians have kept their attention on God with short, frequent prayer. The most common is the Jesus Prayer: "Lord Jesus Christ, Son of the living God, have mercy on me, a sinner." My favorite is: "I love, I adore, I hope, and I trust in you. And I beg pardon for all the times I have not loved, adored, hoped, or trusted in you." You can also take a short phrase from your scriptural prayer or from the Gospel reading of the day and repeat it as it comes to mind.

Meditative Prayer

There are many excellent books on this practice. I find it especially helpful to meditate at the end of the day. My favorite meditation is the scriptural Rosary—a meditative prayer on the life, death, and resurrection of Jesus. I stay away from any form of meditation that does not focus on God.

The Prayer of Quiet

Too often we talk and talk to God, but rarely do we listen. Remember, prayer is a conversation. I find it very difficult to listen unless I'm in a chapel, away from all distractions. I sit before the tabernacle, become very still, and say, "Speak, Lord, your servant is listening." I promise that if you do this, God will speak to your heart. You may not know what he says, but you'll see the fruit. (At the very least, you will learn to be more comfortable with silence, which is important in your work.) Finding a peaceful corner in your own house or a favorite place outdoors where you can pray quietly and listen to the Lord is also helpful.

Spiritual Reading

Life is too short to spend it reinventing the wheel. Consult those who have gone before you on the path. There are many books of spirituality from which to choose. Find an author who speaks to your heart and spend a few minutes each day in meditative reading.

Live in a State of Grace

You cannot be an instrument of God's grace to your patients if you persist in sin. Ask God to show you areas of your life that are not in order. Ask him for a well-formed conscience. Jesus came to comfort the disturbed and to disturb the comfortable. If you pray regularly, sin will cause discomfort to your soul.

Live a Life of Forgiveness

Be quick to ask forgiveness from God, and just as quick to offer it to others. How can you ask your patients to forgive when you won't do it yourself?

Examine your conscience every evening. Ask forgiveness for your sins and acknowledge the good you did badly as well as the good you failed to do. Forgive those who have hurt you during the day. Remember, forgiveness is not a feeling but an act of the will. Then forgive yourself. (I find frequent sacramental confession to be a great source of healing and grace.)

Live a Life of Joy

Finally, play, laugh, and rejoice in every day given to you. As G. K. Chesterton said, "Angels can fly because they take themselves so lightly."

Midwifing souls is God's work. If you're doing it for anyone else, you won't burn out—you'll french fry. When you give all of yourself to four or five families in one day, there's nothing left. Do the math. And what happens the next day? You can't give what you don't have.

If you don't have a strong spiritual life, begin to develop one now. Saint Augustine said, "God is more anxious to bestow his blessings on us than we are to receive them." This work has been a powerful conversion experience for many who came before you.

Once when I had several patients whose pain and sorrow were breaking my heart, I knelt in the chapel, begging

Jesus to bless them. To my horror, I heard deep in my soul, "You are my blessing to them." I had been on the verge of tears, but they came in torrents when I heard that message. "But I'm such a sorry blessing, Lord!" I cried. "Then let me bless through you," he answered.

There are moments—majestic moments—when I get out of the way so that God can bless through me. And there are moments—ugly moments—when I grow lazy and can be indifferent to the suffering Christ before me. But most of the time I'm more or less a sorry blessing.

I sometimes feel guilty for not doing more. When I've been lazy or indifferent, that guilt is justified and I need reconciliation with my patient and my God. But usually the guilt is a product of my pride. How could any human ever do enough for a suffering brother or sister? And we are so human. So be kind to yourself. Some days, when I have a particularly needy patient, the others get a kiss and a promise. If you are attentive, all will receive what they need at their neediest, just like children in a large family.

You have been called to the beautiful vocation of leading God's children safely back to him. If you will persevere in tending the garden of your soul, God will make up for all of your deficiencies. Let him work. Wherever you are on the journey, you will always receive much more than you give.

I pray with Saint Paul for you:

Out of his infinite glory, may he give you the power through his Spirit for your hidden self to grow strong, so that Christ may live in your hearts through faith, and then, planted in love and built on love, you will with all the saints have strength to grasp the breadth and the length, the height and the depth, until, knowing the love of Christ, which is beyond all knowledge, you are filled with the utter fullness of God. Glory be to him whose power, working in us, can do infinitely more than we can ask or imagine; glory be to him from generation to generation in the Church and in Christ Jesus for ever and ever. Amen (Eph 3:16–21).

NINE

※ • ※

The Problem of Suffering

EVEN THOUGH WE HAVE MADE great strides in achieving pain control, we often are not able to relieve all suffering. For unknown reasons, there are some patients whose physical pain simply cannot be alleviated. And even when physical pain is controlled, there is still emotional and spiritual pain. As a midwife for souls, you must come to terms with the problem of suffering or you will not be able to do this work.

The Bible gives us some clues about suffering, and inspired minds have thought deeply and well on this subject. I'd like to share some of their insights with you. But please remember that suffering is a mystery that we will never fully understand in this life.

The Cause and the Cure

The Bible tells us that in the Garden of Eden there was no suffering. God's plan for us was intimacy with him, to walk together in the cool of the evening. Original sin brought suffering and death into the world and has been passed on ever since as a spiritual affliction.

But God didn't just close the door and turn out the lights. Our punishment somehow becomes our cure. Peter Kreeft calls the sacrifice of Jesus "spiritual Judo"—using the enemy's own power against him. Sin, the cause of suffering, is conquered by suffering; death conquers death.[2]

Suffering, a mystery beyond our comprehension, was used to open heaven. Suffering must have infinite value, because instead of taking our crosses away, Jesus embraced his and asked us to imitate him.

He also entered into our suffering and shared our helplessness. "And at the ninth hour Jesus cried out in a loud voice... 'My God, my God, why have you forsaken me?'" (Mk 15:34) No one with faith can ever say to God, "You don't know what it's like to suffer like this!" Jesus has been called the tears on the face of God. He has blessed our suffering and made it holy. The pains of dying become birth pangs of eternal life.

When people ask me, "How can you stand such depressing work?" I tell them that working in labor and delivery would be very depressing if you never saw a baby. Hospice midwives must see the baby, the soul, safely delivered to God, with their spiritual eyes.

"A woman in childbirth suffers, because her time has come; but when she has given birth to the child she forgets the suffering in her joy that a human being has been born

---

2. Peter Kreeft, *Making Sense Out of Suffering* (Ann Arbor: Servant Books, 1986).

into the world. So it is with you: you are sad now, but I shall see you again, and your hearts will be full of joy, and that joy no one shall take from you" (Jn 16:21–22).

In nursing school, I was taught that a good nurse keeps a professional distance so that she can effectively care for the patient and protect herself emotionally. It took me years to discover the truth; the only way to protect yourself from the pain of compassion is to never love. For a midwife of souls, that just isn't an option.

Of all the people who claimed to love Jesus, the Gospel of John tells us that only John, the disciple Jesus loved; Mary, the mother of Jesus; and a few other women had the heroic love to remain at the foot of the cross. It is sheer agony to sit by, helpless, and watch a loved one suffer. But true love won't permit us to turn away; it is more painful to flee than to remain.

When we have lost all thought of ourselves as we share in the passion of another, something wonderful happens to us. In his apostolic letter on human suffering, Pope John Paul II states, "Man cannot 'fully find himself except through a sincere gift of himself.'"[3] At the foot of the cross we are showered with grace. We are gold purified in fire; our souls stretch and become better.

In the children's classic, *The Velveteen Rabbit*, the Rabbit asks if it hurts to become Real. The Skin Horse replies, "When you are Real you don't mind being hurt." He goes on to say, "Generally, by the time you are Real, most of your hair has been loved off, and your eyes drop out and

---

3. Pope John Paul II, On the Christian Meaning of Human Suffering, *Salvifici Doloris* (Boston: Pauline Books & Media, 1984), p. 49.

you get loose in the joints and very shabby. But these things don't matter at all, because once you are Real you can't be ugly, except to people who don't understand."

Working with the dying has taught me to dive in, to love deeply and well. I share their pain, cry with them, and get my hair loved off. Then I rejoice when I have another friend safely in the arms of God. And every time I accompany a soul on that journey, I become a little more Real.

The Question of "Assisted Death"

C. S. Lewis said that kindness without love leads to indifference, even contempt. This is the kindness that leads us to kill animals, to put them out of their misery. The secular humanism that abounds in our society is leading people to rally for this same "kindness" for our sick brothers and sisters. (Ironically, they call this "euthanasia," which means "good death.") The world insists that life only has value if it is productive, and that all suffering is senseless. Christianity teaches that every life has value, and that those who suffer can offer immense spiritual productivity.

In his apostolic letter on human suffering, Pope John Paul II points out this spiritual productivity for the individual, the Body of Christ, and the entire world. He teaches that the suffering person receives special graces, and can be lifted by that grace to spiritual maturity, even greatness, which inspires those around him or her. Pointing to the parable of the Good Samaritan, the pope says that suffering also serves to open our hearts to those who are hurting, to cut through our selfishness and inspire us to loving action.

But when united to the redemptive suffering of Christ, sufferings "constitute a special support for the powers of good."[4] Just as Jesus, nailed to the cross, descended to the depths of human weakness and at the same time was lifted up, so "the weaknesses of all human sufferings are capable of being infused with the same power of God manifested in Christ's cross. In such a concept, to suffer means to become particularly susceptible, particularly open to the working of the salvific powers of God, offered to humanity in Christ."[5]

John Paul II also reminds us that Christ bestowed a spiritual motherhood on the Virgin Mary when he gave her to John, his beloved disciple, "so that every individual, during the pilgrimage of faith, might remain, together with her, closely united to him unto the cross, and so that every form of suffering, given fresh life by the power of this cross, should become no longer the weakness of man but the power of God."[6]

The Presence of Christ

Citing Matthew 25:40, "Truly I say to you, as you did it to one of the least of these my brethren, you did it to me," John Paul II states that "[Christ] himself is present in this suffering person, since his salvific suffering has been opened once and for all to every human suffering. And all those who suffer have been called once and for all to

---

4. Ibid., p. 47.
5. Ibid., p. 36.
6. Ibid., p. 45.

become sharers 'in Christ's sufferings' (1 Pet 4:13), just as all have been called to 'complete' with their own suffering 'what is lacking' in Christ's afflictions (Col 1:24). At one and the same time Christ has taught man to do good by his suffering and to do good to those who suffer."[7]

An atheistic society may argue that the sick and dying have no purpose, but we, as midwives of souls, are eyewitnesses to the infinite value of the last days. We see the miraculous spiritual growth and reconciliations, the heroism, humor, and unconditional love of the dying. We feel the graces that flow and, if we're attentive, we see the eyes of Jesus.

Even if the whole world insists that killing can be an act of mercy and compassion, hospice midwives must stand firmly and boldly in the defense of life, from womb to tomb. It's nothing less than our duty to speak the truth we've been blessed with. From those who are given much, much is expected.

---

7. Ibid., p. 54.

TEN

❦

Harvested Fruit

"And blessed are those who never turned away, and blessed are those who stood quietly in the rain. Theirs shall be the harvest; for them the fruits."

Rainer Maria Rilke
From *The Book of Hours*

PROCESSING YOUR EXPERIENCES will yield valuable fruit that will enable you to be a better midwife. After a person's physical death, take the time to review his or her story. Ask yourself two questions:

"What did this person teach me?"

"If I knew at the beginning how this story would turn out, what would I have done differently?"

Nothing irritates me more than learning a lesson the hard way, then remembering that I'd learned that very same lesson a few years earlier. So I try to write about significant patients and what they've taught me. The act of writing seals them in my memory and gives me insurance against losing my way in the future. Often, when I start walking down a similar road, a patient's story—and the lesson that person taught me—will spring to mind. Or when I'm feeling lost, I can browse through the stories in my memory and find wisdom for the current situation.

When I first wrote this book in 1992, I'd been a hospice nurse for a relatively short time. In the years that followed, I found myself wishing that I could wrap a big red bow around the new lessons I was learning and share them as well. Now, with this new edition of *Midwife for Souls*, I'm delighted to have the opportunity to offer the following stories—and the lessons they contain—as a gift to you and your patients. I hope you will find in them further wisdom for the journey.

❧ ❧ ❧

In every caregiving relationship, there is an imbalance of power between the strong, capable giver and the weak or ill receiver. When you're the caregiver, you don't notice it so much, but the patients are often painfully aware of the absence of reciprocity in your relationship with them. It can be a heavy burden for them to bear.

A normal relationship between two people consists of giving and receiving. Anything you can do to promote normalcy, especially in your relationship, is life-giving to the patient.

Allow Yourself to Receive

Grace could talk the ears right off your head. I could hardly believe that this tiny, elderly platinum blond had a terminal illness as she flounced from room to room during our first visit. She showed me her full-length mink coat, making sure I noticed her name embroidered on the red satin lining. "I've always kept a mink payment instead of a car payment," she said, a sparkle in her eyes. "And I highly recommend it." I heard about her third husband, a man who came to her garage sale...and never left! She shared her whole life story in the first fifteen minutes—always moving, always talking—leaving me dizzy in her wake.

And could she ever curse! It was all I could do not to wince from the steady stream of expletives coming from her mouth. After a while, I ruefully had to admire her fluency. I've never heard anything like it.

Our visit ended abruptly, after she penciled me in on her appointment calendar. Grace made it clear from the beginning that she was queen of her kingdom and in charge of our relationship.

We settled into a routine, which proved highly frustrating for me. I always started out trying to do my job, which included a complete physical assessment, but she had no use for that. "It's such a bore, talking about my health. Let's have fun instead." Then she'd plant herself on the piano bench, pull me down beside her, and pound out dance hall tunes. Other times, she'd cover the couch with squishy pillows and force me to join her for some trashy daytime TV.

But I had a job to do! "Grace, I have to know. Are you having any pain?"

"Honey, I like to keep a little pain. It lets me know I'm alive." Then she'd tell me a dirty joke.

Our visits always ended the same way. I would announce my intention to leave, and Grace would spring one of her planned activities on me. Sometimes it was a cooking lesson. Once we hung all of her pillows on the clothesline to freshen them. More often than not, it was a sing-a-long. She loved to belt out show tunes, and could play just about anything on the piano. If I didn't know the words, she called out songs until she found one I knew. Then we would sing. As a hopelessly musically-impaired individual, I would much rather have eaten a dirt sandwich. But Grace never took no for an answer.

I found myself increasingly frustrated with this arrangement, until I ran across a quote from Sister Wendy Beckett: "Actions fueled by prayer have the radiance of prayer." Aha! I'd found a way to rationalize our visits. So, watching trashy daytime TV with Grace counted as spiritual care. I could live with that.

As time went on, Grace planned our visits with even greater thought and attention to detail. Occasionally, when she was having a particularly good day, she would prepare a meal for me. Bubbling with anticipation, she would lead me to the dining room, and I would find a table immaculately set with her finest linens, china, and crystal. Once she even lit a fire in the fireplace! It was almost physically painful to have a terminally ill woman serving me. But it brought her tremendous pleasure, so I went along.

Then one day, she made a formal pronouncement: "I am not afraid to die." I was shocked speechless, but Grace was never at a loss for words, so she didn't notice.

"Well, I guess I should tell you that I'm not a religious person." (I put on my best poker face for that news flash.) "Oh, I tried to teach myself to be Catholic. I even tried to be a Jew one time. All that stuff just gets in my way. But I am a very spiritual person.

"My neighbor across the street is worried sick about my soul. She comes over here, all mealymouthed, and says, 'Grace, how do you expect God to help you when you take his name in vain?' And I tell her, 'He's God, for God's sake. He knows I'm just kidding!'" She glanced at me sideways. "I told you I'm not afraid to die. Don't you want to know why?" I could only nod.

"I was standing in my kitchen the other day, washing dishes, and having a good old-fashioned pity party. 'No fair. Why do I have cancer?' I felt a tap on my shoulder, but I just ignored it. 'I'm too young to die. Woe is me.' There was another tap on my shoulder, but I just shrugged it away. 'Why me? I'm in the prime of my life.' When I felt the tap on my shoulder the third time, I spun around and hollered, 'What the hell do you want?'" She paused for dramatic effect. "And who was standing in my kitchen but Jesus Christ himself!"

"Grace," I whispered, "only you would say 'What the hell do you want' to Jesus Christ himself!" She laughed and agreed. "And what did Jesus say to you?"

"He called me by name," she said. For the first time, I saw tears in her eyes. "He said, 'Grace, it's going to be okay. Everything's going to be okay.'" She straightened her shoulders and lifted her chin in a confident pose. "And now I feel like he's right here, in my breast pocket—a comforting presence that never leaves. From that moment, I haven't worried at all, about anything." She winked and gave me a sly grin. "But I still give my neighbor hell!"

Grace was a bossy rascal, and one of my best teachers. She demanded that I approach her as a person, not as a patient. She forced me to scrap my agendas and abandon my judgments. She strong-armed me into being the companion she needed. From Grace I learned that sometimes you have to be a willing recipient so that others can experience the joy of giving. I learned that it's impossible to waste time with a dying person. Grace also helped me to remember that God was, and is, and always will be perfectly capable of cultivating souls.

※ ∙ ※

Our knowledge and experience are often great sources of comfort to our patients. Knowing that this is not our first rodeo, that we have tricks up our sleeve, gives patients and their families confidence that we will be their safety net.

Experience can sometimes lead to paternalism, though. We can be overbearing in trying to convince patients and families that what we recommend is the right thing to do, and any other choice is foolish at best. Actually, our job is to provide the best information we have, so the patient and family can make decisions that fit their situation. They have the right to make what we consider to be bad decisions. And sometimes those bad decisions are blessings in disguise.

Allow Patients to Float Their Own Boat

The first time I saw Bob at the hospice house, he was unresponsive and very near death. Without any family members present, there was no way for me to know anything about the person he had been. Over the course of three consecutive nights, I cared for this mystery man.

In the middle of the third night, just as I was giving him medicine by suppository, Bob gave me the scare of my life.

"Do you mind if I ask what you are doing?" he said in a booming voice.

And just like that, Bob re-entered the world of conscious living. For Bob, living meant getting up and around, so he immediately focused all his energies on that goal. He wanted out of that bed in the worst way, but we simply couldn't oblige him. His heart and lungs were in such bad shape; we knew he couldn't tolerate the mildest physical activity. In an effort to protect him from injury, we placed a safety vest on him and tied it securely to the bed frame. (This was in the olden days. We rarely use restraints anymore.)

As it turned out, our determination to keep Bob in bed was only exceeded by Bob's determination to get up. He struggled against that vest during every waking moment. Once I found him exhausted and blue in the face from his efforts. His oxygen cannula was firmly lodged in his left ear and he had worked the safety vest up under his armpits. His legs were sticking out through the side rails, and both feet occupied one leg of his pajamas. Rushing to help, I cried, "What in the world has happened to you?"

In a weary voice, he said, "It's a long, long story."

Shortly after that incident, he pushed the call light and bellowed, "I need to talk to the fire marshal. If this place catches on fire, I'll have to walk out of here with a bed on my back."

His loving daughters had seen enough. They demanded that we release all restraints and let their dad go free. All the nurses were horrified. We painted ghastly scenarios of broken hips and brain injuries, but the daughters wouldn't budge. "We just don't care anymore. He's dying anyway. Turn him loose!"

So we made the daughters sign documents releasing us of any liability for the certain catastrophes to follow. We removed the safety vest, then stepped back and waited for disaster. Bob's daughters put down the side rail and helped him to swing his legs over the side of the bed. With a daughter on each arm, he slowly stood up. And wonder of wonders, he took his first tentative steps. Bob could walk!

With a few days of practice, he was able to prowl around his room at will. But Bob wasn't satisfied. He would come sauntering out into the hallway, only to get whiplashed by his oxygen cord. We added twenty, forty, and then sixty feet of oxygen tubing to satisfy his wish to be at large on the unit.

Eventually Bob even went on outings with his daughters, bringing back "essential" items from his house that he just couldn't live without. Once he returned with a telephone book from the '60s, a two-pound tin of pepper, and a pocket knife. His room started looking like a hardware store owned by a demented shopkeeper. And his sense of humor came back full force, which was a blessing to us all.

One day as I walked into his room, he quickly picked up his Bible, opened it to a random page, and pretended to be engrossed in study.

"Ask me what I'm doing," he demanded, without looking up.

"What are you doing, Bob?" I asked, dutifully playing the straight man.

"Studying for finals!" he crowed, and then laughed for five minutes at his own joke.

The last time I saw Bob, he was unresponsive and very near death. We all took his decline especially hard, because he had worked his way deep into our hearts. Bob had become a friend.

I approached his bedside reverently. Holding back tears, I whispered into his good ear. "When you get to heaven, will you save me a place?"

Clear as a bell, Bob whispered his last words: "Paddle your own dang canoe."

⤝ • ⤞

Some situations are simply beyond our capacity to effect or control. At such moments we are called to bear witness, be still, and know that he is God.

Bow Your Head to the Mystery of Suffering

My partnership with Jess seemed inevitable. She was a well-loved woman, fighting a very public battle with cancer over the course of a decade. Mutual friends conspired for a couple of years to get us together. They would whisper in my ear, "Can't you help Jess? She's in so much pain." And they would whisper in her ear, "What about hospice? They could help you get comfortable."

But Jess wasn't planning to die, thank you very much. At least not anytime soon. She'd outlived the doctors' predictions time and time again, as she met one personal goal after another. Her daughter's wedding had come and gone, and so had her son's ordination as a Catholic priest. But she still had two children left at home in need of mothering, and she had every intention of launching them as well.

We would smile shyly at each other across the church parking lot. Did she guess how I longed to get my hands on her? I could tell she thought of me as one notch above the grim reaper. She kept her distance with determination.

I finally got my chance. The pain must have been close to unbearable, or she would never have agreed to meet me. Grudgingly, she signed onto the hospice program, and I went to work.

"We can get you comfortable," I promised her that first day.

"You are not God, Kathy Kalina," she said.

Jess's pain was the biggest challenge of my life. There were layers and layers of it, and every time we'd get one type of pain under control, another would rear its ugly head. But I kept up the cheerleader routine. "Hang with me, Jess. We can get you comfortable."

"You are not God, Kathy Kalina," she said.

I carried her pain around with me like a boat anchor. I consulted experts, scoured the literature, and dreamed up a new pain management plan every week. "We can do this," I told her. (I was trying to convince myself as well.) "We can get you comfortable."

"You are not God, Kathy Kalina," she said.

Ignoring her tired comment, I began to extol the virtues of yet another new medication.

"No," she said. "Stop messing with my medicine. No more changes." And she meant it.

I was teetering on the edge of despair that night, sitting on my front porch, when I had an epiphany. Browsing through a magazine, these words jumped off of the page and into my heart: "Bow your head to the mystery of suffering."

Jess's pain wasn't a puzzle to solve. This was her journey, and I needed to respect her decisions. No more cheerleading. I vowed to walk with her and provide the help she wanted, not the help I wanted to give.

"I understand that you want me to leave your medicine alone," I told her at our next visit. "But what can I do for you?"

She didn't hesitate to answer. "You can bring me Communion when you come. You can make your visits in the afternoon. You can help me get ready to pick my kids up from school."

After that, she refused to talk about the pain. We had great visits, beginning with a mini-Communion service, sharing food for the journey. She always had her clothes picked out, and we chatted about all kinds of things as I helped her get dressed for her big outing. Then I'd give her a boost into the minivan and pray for traveling mercies as she slowly drove off to the school.

It was a hard lesson, but Jess taught me how to just be with her, a companion on the journey. There was no way to know we were heading straight for a miracle. She met me at the door a handful of days later, grinning like a child at Christmas. "The pain is gone! I'm jumping up and down inside! It's just gone!"

I wonder if her pain was body language for the suffering of her entire being. She had tried to tell me, but I just couldn't hear it. "You are not God, Kathy Kalina." What arrogance to think that I could make it all better. There is no medication for the painful knowledge that you will not live to mother your children.

Jess had a glorious reprieve from the pain. It returned eventually, but it was different after that: manageable, nearly always tolerable, and intermittent. I didn't understand it then, and I don't understand it now. Jess taught me that there's only one proper response to a mystery: Bow your head and acknowledge that he is God (and you are not).

◦

When I started this work, someone told me that unconditional love is a wonderful goal, but at times you have to settle for unconditional positive regard. Every human being is a child of God and worthy of compassion, even if you find yourself feeling that someone is unlovable. Sometimes I have to remind myself that love is not a feeling. Love is action.

Practice Unconditional Love

I liked Ricky's daughter the minute I laid eyes on her. She was a sweet girl in her early twenties who had bootstrapped herself into a decent life, no thanks to her father. "I'm trying to do right by my dad, but he just won't do right." She told me. "He never has and he never will. I can't remember a time when he had a job. He's always been a full-time drug user and a part-time drug dealer. He doesn't care about anyone or anything."

Just the day before, she told me in hushed tones, Ricky had hobbled out of the county hospital hours after surgery on his foot and against medical advice. But then, that was his style. After his kidneys had failed, he had missed so many appointments that the staff at the dialysis center had actually told him not to come back (and they never give up on anyone). Now he had reached the point when treatments were no longer possible, even with his cooperation. His daughter felt duty-bound to get him some help, while keeping a safe distance to protect her own sanity.

After filling me in on his background, she led me into the flophouse Ricky called home. I wouldn't call our brief time together a visit, because he did his best to ignore me. When I tried to explain our program, he said he didn't want nurses to come nosing around his house. Ricky seemed oblivious to the gravity of his situation and the burden his refusal of help put on his daughter. I left shaking my head, wondering what would become of him.

I underestimated his daughter's persistence, because he was admitted to our hospice later that week. I saw him again the night he moved, with the help of our team, from his hovel to a nursing home. He cried like a wounded animal, mourning the loss of his freedom and begging for pain relief. His daughter cried along with him, in spite of herself. He showed up empty-handed, without any of the medications the hospice had supplied days earlier, and his daughter told me that he'd used them to throw himself a party. Ricky just couldn't resist wrecking his own life.

His poor choices left me scrambling to make things better for him. After sending out an impassioned plea to the pharmacist, I managed to get narcotics delivered right away, and his pain crisis was resolved. It was surprisingly difficult for me to be in Ricky's presence. His physical appearance and deficient hygiene would put anyone off, but it was his surly, contemptuous attitude that I found nearly impossible to bear. I left with great relief to respond to another emergency.

The following week, the nursing home staff called me out to see him in the middle of the night. I found him restless and very near death. When I called his daughter, she sounded sad but distant at the news of his decline. I really expected her to come and be with him, but it seemed that his constant neediness and lack of appreciation had left her with compassion fatigue. She told me she'd come by to check on him in the morning. After seeing that he got the appropriate medications, it didn't seem right to leave him alone, so I pulled up a chair.

In that darkened room, alone with Ricky, I felt nothing for him at all. I looked at him and saw self-destruction, and thought of all the pain he had inflicted on himself and those around him during his life. Then he opened his eyes and locked onto mine. If the eyes are the window to the soul, then Ricky's soul was in desperate shape.

I put my hand over his heart and prayed for him. Almost immediately, I began to look at him differently. If I squinted my eyes and gazed at him through "soft eyelashes," I could see through his rough exterior. Another nurse's advice from a similar situation came to mind, and I told myself this story:

"Once upon a time, Ricky was a newborn baby. A young mother held him in her arms and marveled at the wonder of her precious child. She had grand hopes and dreams for him. No one knows how or why he took so many wrong turns, or what led him down the destructive path that brought him to this place in time. But here he is. He's fallen into my lap, and what am I to do? What would I wish for, if a strange woman sat next to my son as he lay dying? I would want her to hold his hand and offer him prayer and peaceful presence in my place."

So that's what I did. After a while, I started praying for Ricky out loud, but softly. It seemed to calm him, so I settled into a steady cadence. Eventually he became totally relaxed, maybe even at peace, and I quietly slipped away.

Midwifing a soul is more often a relay than a marathon. After I did my part, his mother visited the next day, and so did the hospice chaplain. A cousin who had been close to him at one time arrived late that night and sat with him until he died around 2:00 A.M.

Ricky taught me that even the most unlovable person can touch your heart. It just takes prayer, gazing through "soft eyelashes," and a good story to help you recognize the child of God inside.

꿏᎐ᶳ

Near the end of one's life, all of the old masks and social niceties fall away. You are dealing with an authentic human being, and in responding to the person, you must be authentic as well.

Learn How to Pray Out Loud

Mary's Bible was not for show. The leather cover, but-ter-soft from constant handling, and the comments henscratched on the margins of every page, told the story. This book was her life preserver, security blanket, and constant source of nourishment. It was holding together by a thread, just like Mary. She spoke eloquently of her faith and her journey through this final illness. Then I asked "the" question: "Are you married?"

A chill swept the room and her eyes flashed with unexpected hatred. "I'm divorced," she said, spitting the words. "And I'll never forgive that sorry ex-husband for what he did to me or for what his leaving did to my kids."

The expression of so much emotion set Mary off physically, and soon she was fighting for air. I gave her medicine and held her hand as we waited for it to work.

"Please pray for me," she gasped.

I had been praying all along, but I dropped my head and closed my eyes so she would know it.

"Pray for me!" she barked, and then I understood. She wanted me to pray out loud. Her eyes were pleading, and I wanted to explain, "You don't understand. I'm a Catholic girl. We don't make them up ourselves!"

My mind raced as I struggled with our different religious beliefs. What if I said the wrong thing? What if I offended her? What could be worse than an offensive prayer, out loud?

"Pray for me!" she demanded. "I'm dying here!"

I bowed my head and did my best imitation of a Protestant praying. "Dear Lord...," I began, but she cut me off in an instant.

"No, *pray!*" she cried, with the little air she had left. "Really pray!"

So I did. It was like diving into the deep end of a swimming pool, and I half expected to sink like a stone. I prayed, out loud, just making it up as I went along, saying what came to mind. As I prayed, her breathing quieted. Soon she was peaceful again.

"Praying Out Loud" became a ritual for us. Every time I tucked her in at night, I prayed her off to sleep. And every time she had a respiratory crisis, I prayed until the medicine began to work. Prayer and morphine never failed to smooth out Mary's suffering and bring on a peaceful sleep. (Except one particular night...but that's another story.)

It might have taken me years to get up the courage to tackle spontaneous prayer with a dying person, if not for Mary. The first time, the depth of her need left me no choice. After that, our nightly prayer ritual gradually increased my confidence. When the next person came along who needed that same comfort, I felt prepared and less afraid. To this day, praying out loud leaves me a little weak in the knees. But I'm able to do it because I trust the Spirit and I've come to trust myself. And each time, I'm thankful to Mary for teaching me how.

❧

It is frightening to have words coming from somewhere besides your brain. When it happens as an inspiration from the Holy Spirit, you always have a choice. You can stifle the words or let them come. A few times I've pushed the words away; each time I did so, I regretted it. Usually I find the courage to let the words go free, and I've always been glad when I did.

Speak When Inspired

Prayer and morphine always helped to alleviate Mary's suffering and bring on a peaceful sleep, until one particular night. I tucked her in as usual and prayed her off to sleep. Thirty minutes later, she rang the call light. "Can you pull me over?" Another nurse helped me re-position her. We barely got back to the desk when she called again. "Please pull me over."

This went on for hours. We checked her from head to toe and could find no physical reason for her behavior. But she just kept calling. "Pull me over." "Please pull me over." "I need you to pull me over."

We tried every combination of medicine to get her to sleep, but nothing worked. We reasoned with her time and time again. She would agree with our logic, apologize for bothering us, then call again minutes later. "Pull me over."

Around 3:00 A.M., all the nurses were fresh out of patience. "Girls, I'm begging you. Please pull me over." Her voice on the intercom was like fingernails on a blackboard.

I marched down to her room with renewed determination. I was going to get her to sleep once and for all. "Mary, open your eyes," I commanded. "Your nose is on the side rail. We can't pull you over any more. It's physically impossible."

She looked up at me with tears in her eyes. "I know. I can see. But...could you just pull me over?"

There was nothing left for me to do but sit down on the floor and cry...and I almost did. Just then, words began to well up from somewhere deep inside of me.

"Mary, do you remember the first time we met? That night you told me that you'd never forgive your ex-husband as long as you live." As I said the words, I was remembering them at that moment, too, because I had completely forgotten about our first conversation.

"That's right."

Mary's face took on that look of icy hatred I had only seen once before at the mention of her deepest wound. I struggled to continue, because I knew how much it cost her to address this subject.

"Mary, do you think you could forgive him as a damaged human being?" I picked up her Bible and held it out to her. "Do you think you could forgive him, just because Jesus does?"

She considered the proposition as though it was a startling, fresh idea. "You know what? I think I could." She reached for her beloved Word and I placed it in her fragile hands. Then she raised her eyes to the ceiling and said, "Jesus, I forgive that sorry ex-husband because you do." She grinned at me, then melted into the bed. I tucked her in, kissed her on the forehead, and crept out of her room.

The silence that followed was cause for great rejoicing. Five minutes became ten and then twenty. Then an amazing sixty minutes passed without a call from Mary. Feeling very proud of myself, I peeked into her room just for the satisfaction of seeing her asleep, at long last.

Instead, Mary had died.

And then it hit me. I never heard her *real* request. "Pull me over." She spent hours trying to tell us that there was an obstacle in her way. Even though there were no physical signs that death was near, Mary was ready to go and found her way blocked by lack of forgiveness. She was stuck and needed a nudge.

How blessed are we that the Spirit hovers near at the hour of a person's death. And how fortunate we are that God will use any willing, available person as a conduit of grace—even an exasperated, out-of-patience, worn-out me.

꙳ ❦ ꙳

One of the midwife's most precarious tasks is to see that the patient's needs are met, while at the same time making sure that the family has peace about decisions that are made along the way. The family's perception is their reality, and events surrounding the death of a loved one will be remembered for years to come.

Take Care of the Story

The first indication that something was terribly wrong with Joseph could have been disastrous. With no warning at all he forgot how to do his job. His fellow air traffic controllers covered for him, and he immediately sought medical attention.

A couple of weeks later the doctors solved the puzzle of Joseph's frightening symptoms, but the diagnosis held no comfort. For all the wonders of modern medicine, no treatment existed for this devastating, rare disease that was already in its final stages. The hospital case manager called to refer him to our hospice, and also to issue a warning about his family.

"His children are burning up the Internet searching for a cure, no matter how far-fetched. What's worse, they're

trying them all, regardless of cost. We don't know everything they're doing to him, and we don't want to know.
The nurses have a strong suspicion that they're even slip-
ping him off-label, non-FDA-approved medications. This
is going to be a tough one."

Immediately I thought his children didn't understand
the diagnosis. Maybe they just weren't very smart. But people with limited intelligence usually don't have research
skills or disposable income for questionable alternative
treatments. Then I thought that perhaps they were unbal-
anced in some way and prone to magical thinking. But
there were four of them, and what were the odds that they
were all disturbed or "a bit unstable"?

On my way to the hospital, I had a stern talk with
myself. "Every patient and every family is a new universe.
Leave all judgments at the door. Open mind; open heart."
I prayed for strength, courage, and direction.

It was obvious from the first moment of our meeting that
Joseph's children, educated professionals in their early twenties, really didn't want to hear about our hospice program.
They had only entertained the idea because he could no
longer stay in the hospital, and they needed help with his
care. After a few minutes of polite listening, the negotiations
began.

"We're doing magnet therapy," his daughter said defi-
antly. "Will your staff have issues with that?"

"No, that won't be a problem," I said.

She ticked off a long list of unconventional therapies
they planned to continue, and I assured her that we would
not interfere. I found it amazing that they were all in agree-

ment with this course of action. In times of crisis, it's rare to find siblings that single-minded. They were suspicious and reluctant about trusting us with their father's care, but their choices were limited. Seeing Joseph's agitated confusion hurt my heart. I knew that we could provide comfort for him and his family, if given the chance.

"I can see how much you all love this man," I said, "and I understand your need to search for every possible treatment that could help him. I can't promise that we'll be able to accommodate all of the therapies you want to try, because we don't know what those are yet. But I can promise that we will work with you."

"That's all we ask." His daughter took my hand and added, "Thank you for not treating us like we're stupid or insane. We're smart people, and we know that all of these therapies are long shots, at best. But this is our dad, and we have to try everything."

When we moved Joseph to the hospice house, the nurses were guarded and suspicious of the family, and I was worried as well. He was now in our care, which meant we carried the burden of liability if things went terribly wrong. I kept repeating to the staff (mostly for my own benefit), "They're just loving their dad. No matter what they do or ask or try, we need to see the love in it."

Joseph's disease was so aggressive that his condition deteriorated hourly. By the second day, his family stopped all of the Internet-generated treatments. His symptoms challenged our entire team, but we were able to get him to a place of comfort. Because his family found the courage to trust us with his care, we were able to minister to their needs as well.

During his last days, Joseph's children turned their energies to providing peaceful presence for him and support to each other. They brought up photo albums and held a delightful "show-and-tell" marathon for family members and friends. We heard countless stories about the incredible man Joseph had been, and we all marveled at his accomplishments. In just a few days, his family had moved past their frantic search for a cure to a place of calm in the midst of the storm.

That's not to say it was easy. When Joseph left this world, you could hear hearts breaking in the room. But his children were able to carry his stories with them, along with a fitting final chapter.

I think it goes something like this:

"Our dad was the best at everything he ever did, and he packed an incredible amount of living into the years he had with us. When we learned that he had a terrible, rare disease, we searched the world over for anything that could save his life. We did everything in our power to change the outcome, because our dad was the best, and our dad deserved the best. We loved him madly, and we didn't care if the whole world thought we were mad."

It's no small thing to take care of someone's story, because the ending belongs to the family forever. When that story leaves family members with a sense of pride and comfort, it is a priceless inheritance.

⚹

I forget sometimes how powerful the act of pure listening can be. Giving a suffering person focused attention provides the opportunity to tell one's own story and process the pain. Maybe even more important is the silent message listening sends: "You are valued. Your thoughts and feelings are important. You are worthy of my time."

Listen Well

After a particularly busy night on call I planned to drop off my paperwork, go home, and sleep for a very long time. But the phone rang on my way out the office door, and I just had to pick it up.

"I wish my husband was a dog," a woman screamed into my ear. "Then I could take him to the vet and have him put out of his misery!"

The woman rambled on about "mercy" killing, and her words were like an ice pick to my heart. I needed a lot of things at that moment, but a *euthanasia-seeking family member* was not one of them. Sleep deprivation at the end of the shift left me in no condition to handle such a volatile situation. Other nurses would be available in thirty minutes or so, but this case called for immediate action.

It took some doing, but I managed to get the woman's name, her husband's name, and their location. "I'll be right there," I said, trying to keep the weariness out of my voice.

For the longest time I sat in the hospital parking lot. I prayed, "Lord, if anything good comes of this, I'll know you did it, because I'm sitting on dead empty. I have absolutely nothing to offer this woman."

First I checked on the patient. He was in a cozy bed, clean and comfortable, watched over by an attentive nursing staff. There was no response from him; even so, he displayed no signs of pain or distress.

Satisfied that the patient was not suffering in any way, I went to meet his wife. I found her in a small waiting room, pacing like a caged animal. She refused to look at me, but her tirade grew in volume and venom for my benefit. I just stood there until she ran out of steam. Exhausted from raw emotion, she fell back on the couch in a semi-swoon. "What's the use?" she said, grabbing a handful of her own hair. "No one understands what I'm going through."

"I want to understand," I said meekly. "Could you explain it to me?"

She didn't need any more prodding than that. Starting at the beginning, she told me what a controlling man her husband had always been. He demanded perfection from everyone, including the pets. Living with him had never been easy. This was obviously a well-worn tale that I found hypnotic. As the woman catalogued her husband's faults, I struggled to remain awake and maintain an attentive expression, just in case she ever looked at me.

Then the story got interesting. One day, right smack in the prime of his life, her husband collapsed from a heart attack. He was successfully resuscitated, but his brain did not survive. For over a decade she had provided his care—alone.

"You spent ten years giving your husband around-the-clock care, all by yourself?" I asked, incredulous. "I can't even imagine how difficult that must have been."

She smiled and made eye contact for the first time. "Those were the best years of our marriage!"

Suddenly, she had my undivided attention.

"For the first time in our lives, I got to decide when we started our day and when we ended it," she explained. "I got to decide what we ate and when. I even got to decide how we spent our money and where we lived. It was fabulous!"

Now I had the whole picture. After all those years, her husband was now dying, but he was still doing it in slow motion. Once again, he had the upper hand. What a sad story! It would have been very hard to hear this woeful tale even on a good day, and this wasn't a good day.

She went on and on about how frustrated she felt and how she couldn't bear her husband's suffering any longer. I listened for what seemed like an eternity, and then I listened some more. Mostly, I listened because I couldn't think of anything else to do.

When she stopped talking to catch a bit of air, I spoke for the third time. "Do you think it's possible that he's doing this like he's done everything else in his overachieving life? Is it possible that he's attempting a world record for the longest dying?"

"That would be just like him! I've even picked out his funeral music. It's going to be Frank Sinatra, singing, 'I did it my way.'"

We laughed together, and it felt really good. By the end of our visit, which might have lasted two hours, she looked like a different woman.

I never saw her again. From what I understand, she held a peaceful vigil until her husband died a couple of days later. Could it be that the simple act of listening dissolved her suffering, or at least calmed her grasping desire for control? Pure grace.

This story might have turned out very differently if I'd been rested and in full possession of my faculties. Would I have been able to resist inserting my thoughts and my beliefs—or even worse, cutting her off to minimize my own discomfort? This woman only needed two things: prayer and patient listening. And by divine Providence, those were the only two things I had to offer.

⚮

If I had to name the most common fear in hospice work, it would be the fear of saying the wrong thing. And that's definitely a risk, because suffering people are tender all over and easily offended. But we can't let fear keep us away from the work we've been called to do. The secret is to show up and bring your best self. Your best self has enough humility to beg forgiveness from the offended party if you happen to say the wrong thing. Most likely you'll be forgiven.

Be Able to Beg Forgiveness

Driving to a home at the time of someone's death is a very familiar trip for me, but nothing could have prepared me for this. A co-worker went home at lunch to check on her daughter who had been depressed, and found her dead from suicide.

Always the model of responsibility, this woman had called work first to let us know what had happened. Her husband was out of town, and it would take time to rally all the friends and family members who could provide the support she really needed. Without a thought I jumped in the car and raced to be with that grieving mother.

On the way, I dreaded the job of first responder. We were mere acquaintances, and I wished that someone closer to her could fill the position. But I was available, and she needed someone–anyone–just so she wouldn't be alone. Even though I felt painfully inadequate, I knew that I could fill that void until real comfort arrived.

I found her dazed in the front yard, the picture of devastation. Instinctively, I hugged her, and she clung to me like a drowning person to a lifeline. After long minutes, a gracious neighbor opened her home to us, providing a comfortable place to gather. I helped to make phone calls, then sat nearby during the police interview, holding her hand. Gradually, close friends trickled through the door. With each arrival, I breathed easier, relieved to see her receive support from people she loved.

Even in the gravest situations, at some point conversation can limp along, just as a way to fill the time. When she introduced me to one of her friends, who mentioned what a special person she was, I unwittingly responded, "Yes, I work with this dear woman. She takes good care of everyone at our office. She's a wonderful mother to us."

She spun around to face me with a horrified expression. "Don't...EVER...say that about me again. Obviously, I'm NOT a good mother!"

My stomach clenched and all the blood drained from my face. I had committed the grievous error of saying the ultimate wrong thing. Even though I knew for a fact that she was, and is, a wonderful mother, at that moment she felt like the biggest failure in the world. Immediately I begged forgiveness, and we moved on.

Making a mistake like that leaves a mark. I could never think of her, or of that day, without cringing at my thoughtlessness. When I ran into her years later, the memory returned, fresh and painful. We caught up a bit on each other's lives, and then she said, "I'll never forget what happened when you came to me that horrible day; the day my precious daughter died."

"That makes two of us," I thought.

"You held me," she said, her eyes glistening from the memory. "Standing out there in the yard, you just wrapped me in your arms, and that's exactly what I needed. Thank you."

I found it amazing that she remembered what I did that helped, but she either forgot, or pretended not to remember, that what I said had hurt her that day. Either way, I knew that I had truly been forgiven, and for this I am ever so grateful.

<hr>

Nurses are notorious for declaring patients and families to be "difficult" or "dysfunctional," when oftentimes they simply don't want what we are offering. We have to find a way to provide the care that's desired while at the same time avoiding an adversarial response unless the patient's needs are not being met.

Suspend Judgment

"We have a new patient," the admission nurse told me. "At least, I think we do. The family members signed the papers, and I've admitted her to the hospice program, but I'm not sure any of the family understood a word I said."

When I tried to get more information, she interrupted, "I can't explain it. You'll have to see for yourself."

The very next morning, I went to meet this mystery family. A female relative gave me a halfhearted welcome, led me through a crowd of people, and deposited me in the patient's room without a word of introduction. I found Tobie, a ninety-eight-year-old slip of a woman, pleasantly confused and quite comfortable in her hospital bed. I could tell at first glance that she had entered the active dying process, because she had that faraway look in her eyes that I've come to associate with "watching the angel show." She seemed to be having a conversation with unseen guests.

A thorough assessment didn't seem possible with so many family members at the bedside, so I asked if we could all talk in the living room. They made motions as if to follow, but only trickled in a few at a time and pretended to listen to me. Most of them quickly wandered off. The few who stayed became engrossed in a television program. I had the hardest time figuring out who was actually providing her care. I couldn't hold anyone's attention long enough to get a straight answer, and started to wonder whether or not English was their first language. Then I asked a general question addressed to no one in particular: "Has Tobie been confused?"

Immediately one of the male relatives responded with enthusiasm, "Come and see this!" He took me back into Tobie's room, and the others followed. When we'd all gathered at the bedside, the man jumped through the doorway and yelled, "Aunt Tobie! Who am I?"

Tobie turned her attention away from the ceiling to study his face. Then she dropped her eyes and tried her best to bluff. "I know who you are," she said.

"All right, then. Who am I?"

When she couldn't answer, the room exploded with laughter, and Tobie laughed as loud as the rest. During my visit they played their game over and over, and everyone, including Tobie, found it equally entertaining each time.

I managed to finish my physical assessment during an intermission from the "Who am I?" game, but eventually gave up on showing anyone how to provide for her care. I left medicine for pain and restlessness, and wrote out detailed instructions because no one would listen to me. I brought in some supplies, then slipped away unnoticed.

I fretted about Tobie all day because I found the family's behavior so odd, and shared my concerns with the team. The social worker agreed to make a visit with me the next day, and I felt relieved to have the support of his expertise.

On arriving at Tobie's room the following morning, we both just stood back and watched the family interactions in amazement. By that time, they had abandoned the television and were spending all of their time watching Tobie instead. It was a standing-room-only crowd, and the regular waves of laughter gave it a party atmosphere. Tobie, still actively dying, was genuinely delighting in the attention. After a while, the social worker and I stepped outside to confer.

I said, "My first instinct is to say that they are a dysfunctional family. But, really, they're just functional in an alternative way." We agreed that Tobie was comfortable, happy, and well-loved. They weren't giving her any medicine, but she seemed just fine without it.

Still, I found the situation very uncomfortable. Gradually, in talking with the social worker, I discovered the real source of my distress. This family found me unnecessary! My usual routine wasn't working, and it seemed that I had nothing to offer. I couldn't leave without making some contribution, no matter how small, so I went back into Tobie's room.

The crowd had thinned out a little, so I dropped the side-rail on her hospital bed and sat down beside her. I took her hands in mine and felt for the first time how dry and rough they were. They were the hands of a working woman, and they had seen over eight decades of labor. There was a sample of some very rich lotion in my nursing bag, so I took it out and gave her a hand massage. She seemed to really enjoy that, so I took off her socks and gave her a foot massage as well. She moaned approval and swayed back and forth from pleasure. Her delight was contagious. Soon we were both grinning and laughing. The laughter called her family back, so I left them, chuckling on my way out the door.

If I never returned, I don't think Tobie's family would have minded a bit. But that wasn't an option. She was now enrolled in our hospice, which made me responsible for monitoring her care unless and until her legal decision-maker signed her out of the program. Because of Tobie's condition and the unorthodox response of her family, I visited every day. The visits were brief and focused. After making sure her physical needs were met and seeing that she was comfortable, I gave her a hand and foot massage.

Then I praised the family for their efforts, delivered any necessary supplies, and got out of their way.

The new routine worked very well for all of us. The family grew to tolerate my intrusions, Tobie loved the massages, and I learned to accept the peripheral role the family had assigned me. As an unexpected bonus, I acquired some much-needed humility. Tobie died surrounded by love and the sound of laughter. And isn't that a wonderful way to go?

❧ ● ❧

In this work, our job is to lend strength and bear witness. There is a time for action and a time for patient presence. Being human, we tend to settle into our comfort zone and serve from that place. Some of us are all about action, which can lead to overbearing attempts to orchestrate the patient's journey. I tend to err on the side of passivity, which sometimes leaves me with regrets.

Get Bossy Sometimes

How I wish I'd been bossy with Lucille. Her life stopped the moment the doctor said she only had six months to live. She went home and immediately gave away all her clothes and all her shoes. When we met eighteen months later, I found her in a darkened room at the back of her daughter's rambling house. She sat in a chair, with the resigned sadness of a prisoner, waiting to die. She told me that she spent all of her time alone, even when her family returned from work each evening. She found no pleasure in listening to the radio, watching television, or reading. From what I could gather, her most meaningful activity was marking an X on the calendar at the end of each day.

With some gentle coaxing, I tried to interest her in something—anything—that would engage her mind, body, or spirit. But Lucille wouldn't budge. Once she said, "I'd kind of like to go somewhere, but I don't have any clothes. I don't even have shoes. It would be wasteful to buy some. I'm dying, you know." When a person has no hope, I believe it's my job to hope for them. But I found her despair insurmountable, and it left me feeling defeated at the end of each visit.

Patiently I watched, hoping for a breakthrough, as Lucille's time frittered away, and then, one day, she died. A hospice chaplain once told me, "You only die on one day. All the rest is living." Not for Lucille. She spent nearly two years on death row. Such a waste! I promised myself that if I ever saw that happening again, I would get bossy about it.

Tina happened along a few years later. She seemed very near death, and I prepared her children for the possibility that she could die that very night. But she didn't. In fact, every time I saw her she was a little stronger. Her doctor shared my amazement as her improvement continued. Soon she was able to go to the bathroom alone and putter around her room.

Every visit caused me to rejoice. "You're doing so well!" I would exclaim. But Tina didn't share my excitement.

"What am I supposed to do?" she always asked me.

"What do you want to do?" I'd ask in return, but she had no answer.

I started making suggestions, as I had with Lucille, for activities she might find engaging, but she batted away my ideas as quickly as I pitched them her way. The situation started feeling very familiar, and then it hit me. Tina was asking me how she was supposed to behave on "death row," that hopeless place of suspended waiting.

"Do you ever leave your bedroom?" I asked, even though I already knew the answer. "You don't have to stay back here. You can go out into your den. And you don't have to live in nightgowns, either. You can wear regular clothes."

She looked at me over her glasses, eyebrows furrowed, on the verge of protest. I looked right back, stern as any scolding mother, not giving an inch. She didn't say a word.

But that little nudge was all it took. The next time I visited, I found Tina sitting in her den, sporting regular clothes and wearing a very self-satisfied expression. "I'll have you know I gave the dog a haircut this morning." She stopped my standing ovation. "Not so fast. That's all I've done, and it took everything I had."

It was absolutely the worst haircut I've ever seen on a dog, and he was slinking around as if he knew it. She must have taken a swipe at him with the shears every time he ran by her chair. But no matter; Tina was back! Soon she'd taken over all of the dog's care and began managing her own finances. She went on regular outings with her children. Tina found a new way to be "normal." She stopped dying and started living.

I think that if Tina had stayed in her room, she might have died in a matter of weeks. After her re-engagement, she lived several months longer than any of us expected, and she enjoyed that time immensely. On the last day of her life, I asked how she was doing. She shrugged her shoulders, smiled weakly, and said, "I'd rather be shopping."

❧

We want a peaceful death for every person. When things don't go according to the version we've scripted in our head, we can take it personally and try to "coach" the patient into doing things according to our will. That is always a mistake.

Honor the Patient's Journey

Maybe his name was John. He never knew me and I never knew him. But his journey taught me a lesson (please, God) that I'll never forget.

I first heard about him in report one morning. "New admission. Thirty-eight-year-old with end stage AIDS. He's actively dying and has no caregiver, so we'll keep him in the hospital."

Every day we'd hear in report that he probably would not live through the night. We learned more about him as time went by. The situation was worse than "no caregiver." There were no family, no friends, nobody. This man was dying all alone in the world, and he was dying slowly.

His nurse, a novice to hospice work, expressed his dismay every morning at John's survival. "He's got to be waiting for his mom," he reasoned, "but I've spoken with her. She's old, she's poor, and she's sick. On top of all that, she lives in New Mexico. Mama's not coming."

Eventually the entire hospice team adopted him. One by one we'd drop in when we were "in the neighborhood."

His physical appearance was shocking, and he made no response to us at all. There was no sign of pain or distress, though. This was a man at peace.

I wish I could say the same for the hospice team. Being in his presence was a painful experience, and we grew more anxious for him and about him with each passing day. It was torture listening to him take one ragged breath after another. And then he'd stop. We'd watch and wait, beginning to think that it was finally over, when another ragged breath would prove us wrong.

We decided as a team that John was stuck. It seemed to us like a post-mature birth, when the baby just won't come. So we moved into the labor coach mode as the days turned into a week, and then two. There's no telling how many of us slipped into his room throughout those last days, hounding him to "go to the light." There's no telling how many ways he was told that his mother was not coming. And there's no telling how many renditions of "Amazing Grace" he was forced to endure.

He became our project. We tried everything to convince him to let go. Every day his condition deteriorated. I can tell you with certainty that if there had not been moral, ethical, or legal constraints, any member of our team could have fallen for the temptation to give him too much morphine to send him on his way. We were puzzled, frustrated, and exhausted from watching his journey. His minute-by-minute survival was excruciating for us, and we were desperate for it to stop.

One morning I happened to be at the hospital nurse's station when John's nurse came careening out of his room.

He slammed his clipboard down on the desk and announced, "The guy won't die! That's all there is to it. For some reason, he won't let go."

Just then we heard a "clump, clump, clump," as an ancient woman with a walker struggled up to the desk and introduced herself. She was John's mother.

We led her to his bedside. She spoke softly, held his hand, and made her presence known to him in the gentlest possible way. Within minutes, John breathed his last.

Sitting with her as she made funeral arrangements was heartrending. There is nothing sadder than a mother losing her child, no matter what age.

Then, every so often, the grief and the tears would recede, and it seemed like the sun rose on her face. "He waited for me!" she said, over and over. "My son waited for me!"

Our whole team was stunned by the way John's story played out, and embarrassed by our arrogance. I can only imagine what he must have thought as we streamed past his bedside, trying to talk him down from the cross. If he could have spoken, he might have said, "My Mom is coming. I'm tracking her. She's already made it to Tucumcari. Get off my back!"

Who could guess what it cost John to wait for his mother? Hanging onto life by the tiniest thread, not for himself but for her. In retrospect, I've never witnessed such a magnificent gift of selfless love.

What a powerful lesson he taught us! Whenever I hear someone say, "What's taking so long?" I don't hesitate. "There's a reason," I tell that person, "and it's a good one.

We just don't know what it is. Our job is to bear witness
and honor his journey."

And when that person listens, it's like a sweet balm to
an old wound.

こ.•.ン

*Sometimes it feels as if I'm watching through a knothole in a fence
what it might be like to die. I get glimpses here and there, and then I
weave them into an imagined picture. For instance, I had become
convinced that the main reason people cling tenaciously to life when
their body has clearly outlived its purpose is their fear of God's judgment. And then a little boy turned that notion inside out.*

Don't Ever Think It's Easy

Hospice means "a place of rest for weary pilgrims."
Brice, four years old, had traveled a long and arduous road
through half of his life, battling a brain tumor. He didn't
seem all that weary, but his family desperately needed the
rest that hospice can provide.

Brice's presence captivated me instantly. This strikingly
handsome man-child radiated peace. His head pulled to
the left against his shoulder and his voice was very soft;
these were his only outward signs of illness.

During the admission process, Brice said, "I'm going to
play...right now." Then he had a grand mal seizure.
Seizures are always frightening to observe, but watching
and waiting for the medicine to work was almost unbearable. When he came around, his grandmother asked,
"Have you been playing?" "Yes," he answered with a smile.
"Jesus swings me in a swing."

His grandmother pulled me aside and told me that Brice had been in a coma for six weeks after his first brain surgery. Months later he had asked her, "Grandma, do you remember when I couldn't walk and I couldn't talk, and Jesus played with me every day?" She said the seizures were very hard on the family, but for Brice it seemed as if he had been taken away to another place, to frolick with his friend Jesus.

The hospice team was able to get Brice's seizures under control, but as he neared death, every so often he would have a mini-seizure. One particular night, it seemed to me that he was approaching his homecoming. By that time, he'd lost use of his right arm, and it curled up, lifeless, on his chest. Every time he had a mini-seizure, he reached for his grandmother's hand with his good one.

His grandmother coached him beautifully through the night. He seemed very close to leaving, so we tried to keep the room still. I even encouraged his Grandmother to close her eyes so he wouldn't focus so much on her.

There was a long period of quiet resting, and then the atmosphere in the room changed. "Shut up," Brice said. His grandmother and I sat up, shocked. That was completely out of character for him. "Make them shut up," he pleaded with us.

"Who do you want to shut up?" I asked softly.

"They're ugly monkeys, and they're saying mean things to me. And I want them to shut up!"

His grandmother and I exchanged glances. I wasn't sure what she made of that, but I knew what I felt. The hair on the back of my neck stood on end, and I had to act. "Brice, you belong to Jesus," I said. "Anything in this room that doesn't belong to him must scram in the name of Jesus." And with that simple prayer of deliverance, peace returned to the room.

Sensing that he needed help letting go, his grandmother told him, "Next time you have a seizure, don't take my hand. Take Jesus' hand."

When the next seizure began, he raised his lifeless right arm straight up in the air, with his fingers curved as if holding an unseen hand. When it ended, he asked, "Is it really okay for me to go with him?"

"Yes, Brice. It's really okay," his grandmother assured him, again and again.

Finally, he told her, "I'll go, if you go with me."

"I can't go with you," she said. "But I'll be there in a little while."

In a forceful voice, he announced, "Then I'm not going!"

Instead, Brice took a bonus day with his family. The next evening, his condition continued to decline and he became less aware of his surroundings. All at once, he seemed distracted. Prior to that moment, his head was always pulled tightly against his left shoulder. Suddenly, he raised his head and looked over his right shoulder. His breathing accelerated. He looked to his left and back over his right shoulder many times, as if to follow a conversation among unseen guests.

"What's their names?" he asked in a whisper, and waited for a reply. Then he said, "That's a funny name."

His family and I shared this incredible moment, watching one side of an exchange with the other side, straining not to miss one word.

"Look," he said, exasperated. "I have to take my puzzles. I have to take my books." We all stifled laughter, as Brice negotiated the "no luggage" rule.

Several hours had passed since Brice looked at anyone with recognition. Suddenly, he locked eyes with his mother, his grandmother, and his grandfather, each in turn. Then a look flashed across his face that said, "No! I can't leave them!" His grandmother whispered, "Go on, Brice. We'll all be there in a little while."

It seemed to me that the room swelled with prayer, as Brice squinted his eyes at a light we couldn't see. Ever so gently, Brice's spirit left his body. We all held our breath and didn't dare speak or touch him, so as not to call him back.

Almost immediately, I saw lightning. The local paper called it "an electrical storm of the highest magnitude," and it lasted for three hours. Many people who'd been touched by Brice told us later that the storm had awakened them, and that their first thought had been, "Brice is gone."

I like to think that during our tearful goodbye to Brice, a multitude cried out with joy, "Here he comes!" And the heavens lit up, raining blessings upon the parched Texas earth.

Serving as Brice's midwife was an indescribable honor. And it broke my heart. At the beginning of my work in hospice I always held back, reserving a part of myself, for fear that my heart would break. For years I refused to care for dying children because I believed that my heart just wasn't strong enough. By the time I met Brice, I'd had my heart broken before. Years have passed, and I've had my heart broken many times since, doing this work. It's the most amazing thing. Did you know that a heart can get stronger in all the broken places? I used to think it took a strong heart to do difficult things. Now I know that doing difficult things is how you get one.

APPENDICES

ONE

Prayers

Unless otherwise noted, the prayers in this section were composed by the author of this book. They may be used and adapted freely.

PRAYER FOR THE DYING

"Into your hands I commend my spirit." Lord, please give (N.) the faith, hope, and love to whisper these words to you from his (her) heart. Give him (her) the courage to abandon himself (herself) completely to you, and protect him (her) from all temptation. Grant him (her) your peace and the confidence that you will provide tender care and comfort to his (her) loved ones after he (she) joins you. Surround (N.) with your angels, and open his (her) ears to their song announcing your presence and beckoning call. In your holy name we pray. Amen.

Prayer at the Time of Death

Into your hands, Lord, we commend (N.)'s spirit. We lift this dear soul up to you as a child of God and the apple of your eye. Please welcome (N.) into your kingdom, and pour your choicest graces and blessings upon this family in the difficult days ahead. Our Father...

We bless you, (N.), in the name of God the Father, who loved you into existence; in the name of God the Son, who died for your sins; and in the name of God the Holy Spirit, who was poured out upon you in Baptism. Amen.

When I'm praying over a patient, or when there's spiritual distress, I use silent, repetitive prayer. I find such prayers ideal for situations when prayer is needed over a long period of time. If the patient remains in spiritual distress and you are called away, you can pray silently before you leave:

O heavenly Father, I thank you for placing (N.) in my care during his (her) last hours on earth. I have done all I can possibly do for (N.). I now give him (her) back to you and trust in your mercy.

Lord Jesus, lover of souls, please banish all fear from (N.)'s heart, and give him (her) the courage to abandon himself (herself) to you. Only you can judge the condition of (N.) soul. Even so, you are the Savior; I beg you to save.

Holy Spirit, divine Comforter, descend upon this family. Give them peace of heart and trust enough to relinquish their hold on their loved one. Console them in their loss, and dry every tear from their eyes. In Jesus' name I pray. Amen.

Prayer for the Family

Lord Jesus, you promised that wherever two or three gather in your name, there you are in the midst of them. Let this family feel your presence and your deep love for them. Give them confidence that their loved one is in your care, and give them hope in a joyful reunion to come. Divine Physician, pour your love on the wounds of their grief, and accept every tear as a prayer from their hearts. Come, Holy Spirit, divine Comforter, and shelter this family under the safety of your wings in the difficult days ahead. In Jesus' name we pray. Amen.

Midwife's Prayers

O Lord, you are my light and my strength. Watch over me as I minister to the dying. I lift up their suffering of mind, body, and spirit to you. Use me as a channel for your healing power.

Help me to be patient, compassionate, and loving. May your light shine through me in this work.

Take all judgments from my heart, as you are the only just judge. Grant me the grace to see you in the sorrowful disguise of the dying.

Thank you for giving me this beautiful vocation. Help me to keep a smile on my face, so others will see what a great joy it is to serve you. Amen.

Lord Jesus, grant us the grace to imitate your mother, Mary, the first Christian and model for hospice midwives. May we, like her, have the courage to remain at the foot of the cross when others flee in fear; and though our hearts are pierced with sorrow, grant us the deep faith and strong hope to keep our eyes focused on the resurrection. Amen.

CHAPLET OF DIVINE MERCY[*]

Often in this book I've referred to silent, repetitive prayer at the bedside of the dying. Most often I pray the Chaplet of Divine Mercy, because I've found it to be a powerful form of spiritual support at the hour of death.

This prayer is counted out on rosary beads, or on your fingers if you don't have a rosary. On the large bead pray:

Eternal Father, I offer you the body and blood, soul and divinity of your dearly beloved Son, our Lord Jesus Christ, in atonement for (N.)'s sins, and those of the whole world.

On the small beads pray:

For the sake of his sorrowful passion, have mercy on (N.) and on the whole world.

This cycle is repeated five times. Conclude with:

Holy God, holy mighty One, holy eternal One, have mercy on (N.) and on the whole world.

THE ROSARY

This is an ancient form of prayer that can also be used as a silent, repetitive way to offer spiritual support at the bedside of the dying. Some Catholic families might want to pray the Rosary aloud to-

---

* Reprinted from the Diary of Blessed Faustina Kowalska, *Divine Mercy in My Soul* (476), copyright 1987, Congregation of Marians. All rights reserved.

gether, with one person leading the first half of each prayer, while the others respond with the second half. Although most Catholics are familiar with the Rosary, it would be a mistake to assume that all Catholics know how to pray it.

Make the Sign of the Cross with the crucifix; pray the Apostles' Creed:

I believe in God, the Father almighty,
Creator of heaven and earth,

and in Jesus Christ,
his only Son, our Lord,
who was conceived by
the Holy Spirit,
born of the Virgin Mary,
suffered under Pontius Pilate,
was crucified, died and was buried;
he descended into hell;
on the third day he rose again
from the dead;

he ascended into heaven,
and is seated at the right hand
of God the Father almighty;
from there he will come to judge
the living and the dead.

I believe in the Holy Spirit,
the holy catholic Church,
the communion of saints,
the forgiveness of sins,
the resurrection of the body,
and life everlasting. Amen.

On the first bead pray the Lord's Prayer, and on the next three pray the Hail Mary for an increase in faith, hope, and love:

Hail, Mary, full of grace, the Lord is with you. Blessed are you among women, and blessed is the fruit of your womb, Jesus. Holy Mary, mother of God, pray for us sinners, now and at the hour of our death. Amen.

The Rosary consists of five decades of ten beads each, each decade being separated by a large bead. Pray the Lord's Prayer on each large bead, followed by ten Hail Mary's on the small beads. While praying the Hail Mary's, meditate on the different events and mysteries in the life of Jesus and Mary. There are joyful, sorrowful and glorious mysteries, as well as the luminous mysteries proposed by Pope John Paul II. I find the sorrowful and glorious mysteries most appropriate for the dying:

Joyful Mysteries

FIRST MYSTERY	The Angel Gabriel announces to Mary that she is to be the mother of Jesus.
SECOND MYSTERY	Mary visits her cousin Elizabeth.
THIRD MYSTERY	Jesus is born in Bethlehem.
FOURTH MYSTERY	Mary and Joseph present Jesus at the Temple.
FIFTH MYSTERY	Jesus is lost and later found in the Temple.

Luminous Mysteries

FIRST MYSTERY	Jesus is baptized in the Jordan.
SECOND MYSTERY	Jesus performs his first miracle at the wedding at Cana.

THIRD MYSTERY   Jesus proclaims the coming of the Kingdom of God.

FOURTH MYSTERY   Jesus is transfigured on Mount Tabor.

FIFTH MYSTERY   Jesus institutes the sacrament of the Eucharist at the Last Supper.

Sorrowful Mysteries

FIRST MYSTERY   Jesus' agony in the Garden of Gethsemane.

SECOND MYSTERY   Jesus is scourged at the pillar.

THIRD MYSTERY   Jesus is crowned with thorns.

FOURTH MYSTERY   Jesus carries the cross to Calvary.

FIFTH MYSTERY   Jesus is crucified and dies.

Glorious Mysteries

FIRST MYSTERY   Jesus rises from the dead.

SECOND MYSTERY   Jesus ascends into heaven.

THIRD MYSTERY   The Holy Spirit descends upon the apostles.

FOURTH MYSTERY   Mary, the mother of Jesus, dies and is assumed into heaven.

FIFTH MYSTERY   Mary is crowned queen of heaven and earth.

TWO

❧ • ❧

Scriptural Comfort for the Dying and Their Families

It is especially helpful to offer scriptural comfort to devout Christians who are having trials of doubt or fear. Ask if there is a special passage you can read to them. If patients are not verbally responsive, often you can open up their personal Bible and find the dog-eared pages or underlined passages they love. If there is no Bible around, perhaps there is a favorite prayer book with special prayers marked.

The Word of God is alive and can touch patients and their families in a profound way. As with other forms of prayer, be gentle and use discretion.

SUFFERING

Turn to me and be gracious to me,
for I am lonely and afflicted.
Relieve the troubles of my heart,
and bring me out of my distress.

Consider my affliction and my trouble,
and forgive all my sins. (Ps 25:16–18)

❦ ● ❧

So we do not lose heart. Even though our outer nature is wasting away, our inner nature is being renewed day by day. For this slight momentary affliction is preparing us for an eternal weight of glory beyond all measure, because we look not at what can be seen but at what cannot be seen; for what can be seen is temporary, but what cannot be seen is eternal. (2 Cor 4:16–18)

❦ ● ❧

Beloved, do not be surprised at the fiery ordeal that is taking place among you to test you, as though something strange were happening to you. But rejoice insofar as you are sharing Christ's sufferings, so that you may also be glad and shout for joy when his glory is revealed. (1 Pet 4:12–13)

❦ ● ❧

For all who are led by the Spirit of God are children of God. For you did not receive a spirit of slavery to fall back into fear, but you have received a spirit of adoption. When we cry, "Abba! Father!" it is that very Spirit bearing witness with our spirit that we are children of God, and if children, then heirs, heirs of God and joint heirs with Christ—if, in fact, we suffer with him so that we may also be glorified with him. I consider that the sufferings of this present time are not worth comparing with the glory about to be revealed to us. (Rom 8:14–18)

ॐ•ॐ

Blessed be the God and Father of our Lord Jesus Christ, the Father of mercies and the God of all consolation, who consoles us in all our affliction, so that we may be able to console those who are in any affliction with the consolation with which we ourselves are consoled by God. For just as the sufferings of Christ are abundant for us, so also our consolation is abundant through Christ. (2 Cor 1:3–5)

ॐ•ॐ

And after you have suffered for a little while, the God of all grace, who has called you to his eternal glory in Christ, will himself restore, support, strengthen, and establish you. (1 Pet 5:10)

ॐ•ॐ

We know that the whole creation has been groaning in labor pains until now; and not only the creation, but we ourselves, who have the first fruits of the Spirit, groan inwardly while we wait for adoption, the redemption of our bodies. For in hope we were saved. Now hope that is seen is not hope. For who hopes for what is seen? But if we hope for what we do not see, we wait for it with patience. (Rom 8:22–25)

ॐ•ॐ

Likewise the Spirit helps us in our weakness; for we do not know how to pray as we ought, but that very Spirit intercedes with sighs too deep for words. And God, who searches the heart, knows what is the mind of the Spirit, because the Spirit intercedes for the saints according to the will of God. (Rom 8:26–27)

HOPE

You who fear the LORD, wait for his mercy;
do not stray, or else you may fall.
You who fear the LORD, trust in him,
and your reward will not be lost.
You who fear the LORD, hope for good things,
for lasting joy and mercy.
Consider the generations of old and see:
has anyone called upon him and been neglected?
For the LORD is compassionate and merciful;
he forgives sins and saves in time of distress.
(Sir 2:7–11)

The LORD is my shepherd, I shall not want.
He makes me lie down in green pastures;
he leads me beside still waters;
he restores my soul.
He leads me in right paths
for his name's sake.

Even though I walk through the darkest valley,
I fear no evil;

for you are with me;
your rod and your staff–
they comfort me.

You prepare a table before me
in the presence of my enemies;
you anoint my head with oil;
my cup overflows.

Surely goodness and mercy shall follow me
all the days of my life,
and I shall dwell in the house of the LORD
my whole life long. (Ps 23)

You who live in the shelter of the Most High,
who abide in the shadow of the Almighty,
will say to the LORD,
"My refuge and my fortress;
my God, in whom I trust."
For he will deliver you from the snare of the fowler
and from the deadly pestilence;
he will cover you with his pinions,
and under his wings you will find refuge;
his faithfulness is a shield and buckler. (Ps 91:1–4)

For I know that my Redeemer lives,
and that at the last he will stand upon the earth;
and after my skin has been thus destroyed,
then in my flesh I shall see God,

whom I shall see on my side,
and my eyes shall behold, and not another.
(Job 19:25–27a)

⟡

Those who love me, I will deliver;
I will protect those who know my name.
When they call to me, I will answer them;
I will be with them in trouble,
I will rescue them and honor them.
With long life I will satisfy them,
and show them my salvation. (Ps 91:14–16)

⟡

Jesus said to her, "I am the resurrection and the life. Those who believe in me, even though they die, will live." (Jn 11:25)

⟡

What then are we to say about these things? If God is for us, who is against us? He who did not withhold his own Son, but gave him up for all of us, will he not with him also give us everything else? Who will bring any charge against God's elect? It is God who justifies. Who is to condemn? It is Christ Jesus, who died, yes, who was raised, who is at the right hand of God, who indeed intercedes for us. Who will separate us from the love of Christ? Will hardship, or distress, or persecution, or famine, or nakedness, or peril, or sword? As it is written,

"For your sake we are being killed all day long;
we are accounted as sheep to be slaughtered."

No, in all these things we are more than conquerors through him who loved us. For I am convinced that neither death, nor life, nor angels, nor rulers, nor things present, nor things to come, nor powers, nor height, nor depth, nor anything else in all creation, will be able to separate us from the love of God in Christ Jesus our Lord. (Rom 8:31–39)

The saying is sure:

If we have died with him, we will also live with him; if we endure, we will also reign with him. (2 Tim 2:11)

Beloved, I do not consider that I have made it my own; but this one thing I do: forgetting what lies behind and straining forward to what lies ahead, I press on toward the goal for the prize of the heavenly call of God in Christ Jesus. (Phil 3:13–14)

Since, then, we have a great high priest who has passed through the heavens, Jesus, the Son of God, let us hold fast to our confession. For we do not have a high priest who is unable to sympathize with our weaknesses, but we have one who in every respect has been tested as we are, yet without sin. Let us therefore approach the throne of grace with boldness, so that we may receive mercy and find grace to help in time of need. (Heb 4:14–16)

⚜

And we have seen and do testify that the Father has sent his Son as the Savior of the world. God abides in those who confess that Jesus is the Son of God, and they abide in God. (1 Jn 4:15–16)

FEAR

Strengthen the weak hands,
and make firm the feeble knees.
Say to those who are of a fearful heart,
"Be strong, do not fear!
Here is your God.
He will come with vengeance,
with terrible recompense.
He will come and save you."
Then the eyes of the blind shall be opened,
and the ears of the deaf unstopped;
then the lame shall leap like a deer,
and the tongue of the speechless sing for joy.
For waters shall break forth in the wilderness,
and streams in the desert. (Is 35:3–6)

⚜

Look to him, and be radiant;
so your faces shall never be ashamed.

This poor soul cried, and was heard by the Lord,
and was saved from every trouble.
The angel of the LORD encamps
around those who fear him, and delivers them.
O taste and see that the LORD is good;
happy are those who take refuge in him.
O fear the LORD, you his holy ones,
for those who fear him have no want. (Ps 34:5–10)

❦

So we have known and believe the love that God has for us. God is love, and those who abide in love abide in God, and God abides in them. Love has been perfected among us in this: that we may have boldness on the day of judgment, because as he is, so are we in this world. There is no fear in love, but perfect love casts out fear; for fear has to do with punishment, and whoever fears has not reached perfection in love. (1 Jn 4:16–18)

❦

I lift up my eyes to the hills—
from where will my help come?
My help comes from the LORD,
who made heaven and earth.

He will not let your foot be moved;
he who keeps you will not slumber.
He who keeps Israel
will neither slumber nor sleep.

The Lord is your keeper;
the LORD is your shade at your right hand.
The sun shall not strike you by day,
nor the moon by night.

The LORD will keep you from all evil;
he will keep your life.
The LORD will keep
your going out and your coming in
from this time on and forevermore. (Ps 121)

When this perishable body puts on imperishability, and this mortal body must put on immortality, then the saying that is written will be fulfilled:

"Death has been swallowed up in victory."
"Where, O death, is your victory?
Where, O death, is your sting?" (1 Cor 15:54–55)

FORGIVENESS

Come now, let us argue it out,
says the Lord:
though your sins are like scarlet,
they shall be like snow;
though they are red like crimson,
they shall become like wool.
If you are willing and obedient,
you shall eat the good of the land. (Is 1:18–19)

Happy are those whose transgression is forgiven,
whose sin is covered.
Happy are those to whom the LORD imputes
    no iniquity,
and in whose spirit there is no deceit.

While I kept silence, my body wasted away
through my groaning all day long.
For day and night your hand was heavy upon me;
my strength was dried up as by the heat of summer.

Then I acknowledged my sin to you,
and I did not hide my iniquity;
I said, "I will confess my transgressions to
    the LORD,"
and you forgave the guilt of my sin. (Ps 32:1–5)

༺ ⚬ ༻

Bless the LORD, O my soul,
and do not forget all his benefits—
who forgives all your iniquity,
who heals all your diseases,
who redeems your life from the Pit,
who crowns you with steadfast love
    and mercy. (Ps 103:2–4)

༺ ⚬ ༻

Good and upright is the LORD;
therefore he instructs sinners in the way.
He leads the humble in what is right,
and teaches the humble his way.

All the paths of the LORD are steadfast love
    and faithfulness,
for those who keep his covenant and his decrees.
For your name's sake, O LORD,
pardon my guilt, for it is great. (Ps 25:8–11)

⋇

For if these things are yours and are increasing among
you, they keep you from being ineffective and unfruitful in
the knowledge of our Lord Jesus Christ. For anyone who
lacks these things is nearsighted and blind, and is forgetful
of the cleansing of past sins. (2 Pet 1:8–9)

⋇

To you, O Lord, I lift up my soul.
O my God, in you I trust;
do not let me be put to shame;
do not let my enemies exult over me.
Do not let those who wait for you be put
    to shame;
let them be ashamed who are wantonly
    treacherous.

Make me to know your ways, O Lord;
teach me your paths.
Lead me in your truth, and teach me,
for you are the God of my salvation;
for you I wait all day long.

Be mindful of your mercy, O Lord, and of
    your steadfast love,

for they have been from of old.
Do not remember the sins of my youth or
    my transgressions;
according to your steadfast love remember me,
for your goodness' sake, O Lord! (Ps 25:1–7)

The Lord is merciful and gracious,
slow to anger and abounding in steadfast love.
He will not always accuse,
nor will he keep his anger forever.
He does not deal with us according to our sins,
nor repay us according to our iniquities.
For as the heavens are high above the earth,
so great is his steadfast love toward those who
    fear him;
as far as the east is from the west,
so far he removes our transgressions from us.
As a father has compassion for his children,
so the Lord has compassion for those who fear him.
For he knows how we were made;
he remembers that we are dust. (Ps 103:8–14)

"Which one of you, having a hundred sheep and losing one of them, does not leave the ninety-nine in the
wilderness and go after the one that is lost until he finds it?
When he has found it, he lays it on his shoulders and
rejoices. And when he comes home, he calls together his

friends and neighbors, saying to them, "Rejoice with me, for I have found my sheep that was lost." Just so, I tell you, there will be more joy in heaven over one sinner who repents than over ninety-nine righteous persons who need no repentance." (Lk 15:4–7)

Psalm 51

The Miserere: Prayer of Repentance

Have mercy on me, O God,
according to your steadfast love;
according to your abundant mercy
blot out my transgression.
Wash me thoroughly from my iniquity,
and cleanse me from my sin.

For I know my transgressions,
and my sin is ever before me.
Against you, you alone, have I sinned,
and done what is evil in your sight,
so that you are justified in your sentence
and blameless when you pass judgment.
Indeed, I was born guilty,
a sinner when my mother conceived me.

You desire truth in the inward being;
therefore teach me wisdom in my secret heart.
Purge me with hyssop, and I shall be clean;
wash me, and I shall be whiter than snow.
Let me hear joy and gladness;
let the bones that you have crushed rejoice.
Hide your face from my sins,
and blot out all my iniquities.

Create in me a clean heart, O God,
and put a new and right spirit within me.
Do not cast me away from your presence,
and do not take your holy spirit from me.
Restore to me the joy of your salvation,
and sustain in me a willing spirit.

Then I will teach transgressors your ways,
and sinners will return to you.
Deliver me from bloodshed, O God,
O God of my salvation,
and my tongue will sing aloud of your
    deliverance.

O LORD, open my lips,
and my mouth will declare your praise.
For you have no delight in sacrifice;
if I were to give a burnt offering, you would
    not be pleased.
The sacrifice acceptable to God is a broken spirit;
a broken and contrite heart, O God, you will not
    despise.

Do good to Zion in your good pleasure;
rebuild the walls of Jerusalem,
then you will delight in right sacrifices,
in burnt offerings and whole burnt offerings;
then bulls will be offered on your altar.

HEAVEN

But the souls of the righteous are in the hand of God,
and no torment will ever touch them.
In the eyes of the foolish they seemed to have died,

and their departure was thought to be a disaster,
and their going from us to be their destruction;
but they are at peace.
For though in the sight of others they were punished,
their hope is full of immortality.
Having been disciplined a little, they will receive
    great good,
because God tested them and found them worthy
    of himself;
like gold in the furnace he tried them,
and like a sacrificial burnt offering he accepted
    them.
In the time of their visitation they will shine forth,
and will run like sparks through the stubble.
They will govern nations and rule over peoples,
and the LORD will reign over them forever.
Those who trust in him will understand truth,
and the faithful will abide with him in love,
because grace and mercy are upon his holy ones,
and he watches over his elect. (Wis 3:1–9)

⁂

"Let not your hearts be troubled; believe in God,
believe also in me. In my Father's house are many rooms;
if it were not so, would I have told you that I go to prepare a place for you? And when I go and prepare a place
for you, I will come again and will take you to myself, that
where I am you may be also." (Jn 14:1–3)

⁂

But our citizenship is in heaven, and it is from there that we are expecting a Savior, the Lord Jesus Christ. He will transform the body of our humiliation that it may be conformed to the body of his glory, by the power that also enables him to make all things subject to him. (Phil 3:20–21)

Blessed be the God and Father of our Lord Jesus Christ! By his great mercy he has given us a new birth into a living hope through the resurrection of Jesus Christ from the dead, and into an inheritance that is imperishable, undefiled, and unfading, kept in heaven for you, who are being protected by the power of God through faith for a salvation ready to be revealed in the last time. (1 Pet 1:3–5)

Then I saw a new heaven and a new earth; for the first heaven and the first earth had passed away, and the sea was no more. And I saw the holy city, the new Jerusalem, coming down out of heaven from God, prepared as a bride adorned for her husband. And I heard a loud voice from the throne saying,

"See, the home of God is among mortals.
He will dwell with them as their God;
they will be his peoples,
and God himself will be with them;
he will wipe every tear from their eyes.
Death will be no more;

mourning and crying and pain will be no more,
for the first things have passed away."

And the one who was seated on the throne said, "See, I am making all things new." Also he said, "Write this, for these words are trustworthy and true." Then he said to me, "It is done! I am the Alpha and the Omega, the beginning and the end. To the thirsty I will give water as a gift from the spring of the water of life. Those who conquer will inherit these things, and I will be their God and they will be my children." (Rev 21:1–7)

"Listen! I am standing at the door, knocking; if you hear my voice and open the door, I will come in to you and eat with you, and you with me. To the one who conquers I will give a place with me on my throne, just as I myself conquered and sat down with my Father on his throne." (Rev 3:20–21)

BOOKS & MEDIA

The Daughters of St. Paul operate book and media centers at the following addresses. Visit, call, or write the one nearest you today, or find us at www.paulinestore.org.

CALIFORNIA

3908 Sepulveda Blvd, Culver City, CA 90230   310-397-8676
3250 Middlefield Road, Menlo Park, CA 94025   650-562-7060

FLORIDA

145 S.W. 107th Avenue, Miami, FL 33174   305-559-6715

HAWAII

1143 Bishop Street, Honolulu, HI 96813   808-521-2731

ILLINOIS

172 North Michigan Avenue, Chicago, IL 60601   312-346-4228

LOUISIANA

4403 Veterans Memorial Blvd, Metairie, LA 70006   504-887-7631

MASSACHUSETTS

885 Providence Hwy, Dedham, MA 02026   781-326-5385

MISSOURI

9804 Watson Road, St. Louis, MO 63126   314-965-3512

NEW YORK

115 E. 29th Street, New York City, NY 10016   212-754-1110

SOUTH CAROLINA

243 King Street, Charleston, SC 29401   843-577-0175

TEXAS

No book center; for parish exhibits or outreach evangelization, contact: 210-569-0500, or SanAntonio@paulinemedia.com, or P.O. Box 761416, San Antonio, TX 78245

VIRGINIA

1025 King Street, Alexandria, VA 22314   703-549-3806

CANADA

3022 Dufferin Street, Toronto, ON M6B 3T5   416-781-9131

¡También somos su fuente para libros, videos y música en español!